D1516944

the series on school re

Patricia A. Wasley
University of Washington

Ann Lieberman
Senior Scholar, Stanford University

Joseph P. McDonald
New York University

SERIES EDITORS

the series on school reform, *continued*

Leading Educational Change

Global Issues, Challenges, and Lessons on Whole-System Reform

Edited by

Helen Janc Malone

Foreword by Michael Fullan

Teachers College
Columbia University
New York and London

Some chapters in this book have appeared in earlier forms in other publications. Permissions information can be found at the bottom of chapter opening pages.

Published by Teachers College Press, 1234 Amsterdam Avenue, New York, NY 10027

Library of Congress Cataloging-in-Publication Data

Malone, Helen Janc.
    Leading educational change: global issues, challenges, and lessons on whole-
      system reform / Helen Janc Malone.
        pages cm. – (School reform)
    Includes bibliographical references and index.
    ISBN 978-0-8077-5473-3 (pbk. : alk. paper)
        1. Educational change. 2. Educational planning. 3. Educational innovations.
    I. Title.
    LB2806.M2234 2013
    370.1–dc23   2013026920

ISBN 978-0-8077-5473-3 (paper)
eISBN 978-0-8077-7264-5

Printed on acid-free paper
Manufactured in the United States of America

20 19 18 17 16 15 14 13   8 7 6 5 4 3 2 1

Dedicated to
the American Educational Research Association
Educational Change Special Interest Group

Contents

PART II: IMPROVING PRACTICE

PART III: EQUITY AND EDUCATIONAL JUSTICE

Foreword

The single word that comes to mind when reading this compendium of short articles on system-wide reform is *fresh*. There is a quality about these chapters that comes across as if you encountered the authors on a given day and asked them to give a spontaneous response to a given question on the topic of education reform. What you get is 25 distinct contributions across five big themes: Emerging Issues, Improving Practice, Equity and Educational Justice, Accountability and Assessment, and Whole-System Change. The book is symmetrical, with five chapters in each part. This is a book on change that you can feast on: Take any of the five parts, read its set of chapters, and draw some new conclusions about the domain of change in question.

The chapters address issues in 15 different countries. We get a range of ideas that makes you sit back and think about the dilemmas, policies, actions, and outcomes of so many strategies operating under different countries. *Leading Educational Change* neither provides solutions nor confuses the reader. What it does do is make you think. It is the equivalent of coming up with new ideas by "taking a shower"—to get away from the problem of change directly and let your mind wander. My advice, then, is to read Helen Janc Malone's compendium as if you were taking a shower. Open your mind and read the chapters, perhaps one part at a time, and see what ideas about leading change emerge indirectly. My guess is that you will be rewarded with new ideas and new ways of thinking about educational change.

In our current work on change we are finding age-old problems being reconsidered in new ways. Top-down change doesn't work, but neither does bottom-up. It is in fact the wrong question. A better question is how do new, good ideas find their way across the whole system. If you are sitting at the center, this leads you to consider how to tap into the ideas and energies of the bottom (schools and communities) and of the middle (districts and regions). Wherever you are situated, you realize that leadership can and must come from any and all levels. This kind of thinking leads us to question what leadership looks like from the middle (districts and regions), and if it can be a force for whole-system change by helping to transform other parts of the middle through lateral networks, or through two-way partnerships with the bottom and the top. We are also finding that the role of technology is liberating possibilities, even as it presents new problems. Change knowledge will never be more needed than it will be in the next few years. We will need new theories of learning and pedagogy, and indeed new theories of change. The chapters in this book will serve as great background to the next phase of reform as they stimulate questions and lines of thought.

Having studied and participated in change efforts from all angles over half a century, I am convinced that the most powerful change process gets inside "the human condition." The two most prominent motivators related to humans are (1) intrinsic motivation–doing something deeply meaningful, and (2) linking with others doing something central to the group where peers are engaged in an effort that is worth doing. How to activate individual and peer motivation on a large scale is the holy grail of change. Read each chapter in this book from the perspective of how ideas tap into the human condition to motivate participation in the process of change.

Dr. Malone's book is indeed a world tour of ideas in education reform, and you will find many ideas about motivation and large-scale change. Read the book and form your own theory of change suitable to your context. You will be rewarded directly (by finding solutions that connect to your own real-world situation), and indirectly (by spin-off insights). You won't find a better book on whole-system change that covers so much ground in such an accessible form than *Leading Educational Change*!

–Michael Fullan, Professor Emeritus, OISE, University of Toronto

Introduction

In the spring of 2011, while attending a U.S. national education conference, between plenary sessions I engaged in a conversation with a school district professional development trainer. Over the course of our discussion, she shared with me her desire to inform teachers and principals in her district about global educational perspectives on system reform and school improvement, but aired her frustration about a lack of succinct literature on this topic that front-line staff could access and easily read during their limited available time.

On my way home from the conference I came up with a challenge: ask foremost education leaders from around the globe to address the current research, policies, and practices that are changing educational systems in 1,500 engaging and compelling words. The authors featured in this volume responded to my challenge to offer brief, captivating, and provocative ideas designed to appeal to practitioners and decisionmakers alike, to all who directly or indirectly shape children's and adolescents' learning experiences. The authors represent fifteen countries across six continents. They are current and former government officials in the ministries of education, directors of international and national education organizations, scholars, practitioners, educational leaders and innovators, and recipients of the most prestigious honors bestowed on thought leaders in the field of education.

Introducing the Five Lines of Inquiry

The development of the educational change knowledge base has grown substantially over the past decade. International assessments, comparative analyses, and diverse capacity-building strategies have led to significant knowledge creation and mobilization within the field. Today, we are beginning to understand in a more nuanced way the intricacies of leading educational change. What we have learned is that we must attend to inputs and outputs equally and address contextual factors and underlying conditions that promote student learning and educational success.

Reflective of the burgeoning knowledge base, this book is organized into Parts that explore five lines of inquiry, each of which offers a brief introduction, situates the thematic discourse, and introduces the chapters contained therein:

> **Part I: Emerging Issues in Educational Change** examines cross-cutting issues that play a role in shaping system-level change.
>
> **Part II: Improving Practice** profiles strategies that build professional capacity and collective inquiry.
>
> **Part III: Equity and Educational Justice** critically analyzes contextual factors that lead to inequitable systems of schooling and considers strategies that promote educational justice.
>
> **Part IV: Accountability and Assessment Systems** attends to the use of internal and external accountability mechanisms as drivers for data-based decisionmaking.
>
> **Part V: Whole-System Change** offers lessons from emerging and established models engaged in comprehensive system-level change.

The five themes are intertwined and represent diverse levers that can be pulled to create meaningful and sustainable change. The chapter authors draw attention to the reality that leading educational change is multifaceted, political, and uncertain but that positive educational change is possible when it is embedded in a clear vision, strong leadership, resource investment, internal and external accountability, high-quality practice, collaboration, and continuous engagement by all stakeholders.

The purpose of this contemporary anthology is to bring to the forefront the latest thinking across the five lines of inquiry in order to promote important discussions, analyses, and innovations within the education sector. Accompanying the book is an Instructor's Guide, available on the Teachers College Press website (www.teacherscollegepress.com), which offers thought-provoking questions arranged by chapters across the five parts that can be used to lead professional development training, classroom instruction, and individual learning, and to generate broader discussions about leading educational change. This book is geared toward education decisionmakers and leaders, practitioners, and policymakers interested in international education and system-level change.

Acknowledgments

This book was realized through the tremendously supportive mentorship of Ann Lieberman, Andy Hargreaves, Alma Harris, and Dennis Shirley, who have guided me throughout the book's writing process and so kindly contributed to this volume. I would also like to thank Michael Fullan for his gracious Foreword and extend my appreciation to the international roster of top education leaders in the field who have authored thought-provoking pieces for this edited compilation. The American Educational Research Association Educational Change Special Interest Group was the core inspiration for this anthology, and I thank its members for their support and continuous commitment to educational change. Personally, I would like to thank my husband Christian and my son Calvin Alexander for their unconditional love and support.

PART I

EMERGING ISSUES IN EDUCATIONAL CHANGE

Educational change is both a process and a set of practices that inform, reform, and redesign systems of education. What constitutes educational change is contextual and dependent on a range of factors that ultimately influence teaching and learning. International benchmarking and standardized assessments, coupled with a growing evidence-base about effective instructional practices and system-level reform, are increasingly influencing how the field approaches educational change in the 21st century.

This Part serves to address five cross-cutting themes that play a critical role in leading educational change: (a) the influence of international assessments on educational policymaking; (b) the uses and misuses of benchmarking as a key lever of educational reform; (c) the tradeoffs associated with standardization of knowledge; (d) the optimal utilization of technology in the learning process; and (e) the benefits of engaging diverse stakeholders in educational decisionmaking.

The book opens with Andreas Schleicher's Chapter 1, "International Comparisons as a Lever for Policy Reform." The author calls attention to the power that international tests such as the Programme for International Student Assessment (PISA) have had in leading macro-level educational policymaking and improvement. Schleicher offers four ways in which PISA has influenced system-level educational change. PISA has: (a) put national goals into a global perspective; (b) identified different approaches to existing practices and policies; (c) measured educational progress; and (d) applied pressure on the political processes to realize educational change. He concludes that PISA has become a powerful instrument used to compare countries' educational performances and to spark reform and innovation within the education sector.

Juxtaposed to the discussion about the significant role PISA has had on educational change is Andy Hargreaves's contribution, "Teleporting

Change: The Dynamics and Distortions of International Benchmarking."
In Chapter 2, he draws attention to four strategies that distort or deny
international benchmarking, a method for improving existing practice:
(a) bench warming, (b) bench pressing, (c) teleporting, and (d) cherry
picking. Hargreaves concludes the chapter by identifying nine factors that
underpin success within and across educational systems, arguing that what
benefits countries is an investment in learning at the school, education
system, and national levels.

Yong Zhao further examines educational change patterns of large
systems by profiling the U.S. and Chinese approaches to reform in Chapter
3, "Directions of Change: Why the United States and China Are Moving in
Opposite Directions." He questions the contextual factors that have moved
the United States toward standardization and China toward innovation
and diversification. Zhao warns the United States to move away from a
test-oriented culture and to nurture creativity and entrepreneurship that is
fitting of the 21st-century learning environment.

Chapter 4, "Mindful Teaching with Technology: Steps Toward
Harmonization," by Dennis Shirley, addresses the role technology plays
in 21st-century education by examining four positions that educators
assume in regard to technology– to endorse it, to question it, to shelter
students from it, or to harmonize with it. The author presents an argument
in support of harmonization as a compromise that balances the use of
technology with deep learning.

Concluding the Part is Chapter 5, "From the Periphery to the Center:
Broadening the Educational Change Discourse," by Helen Janc Malone,
the book's editor. This chapter draws attention to four considerations
that are largely absent from educational change discussions: the need to
(a) broaden discourse about the purposes of education beyond the labor
market arguments, (b) focus on student-centered learning; (c) recognize
the role outside-of-school learning plays in supporting student education,
and (d) engage front-line stakeholders–teachers, parents, students, and
community members–in leading educational change. The author argues
that the four elements are necessary in order to widen the conversation on
how to create and nurture authentic learning experiences for all students
and how to lead meaningful educational change.

CHAPTER 1

International Comparisons as a Lever for Policy Reform

Andreas Schleicher

The Programme for International Student Assessment (PISA), launched in 2000 by the Organisation for Economic Co-operation and Development (OECD) to observe learning outcomes among the world's major economies, has become a global tool used to compare progress across educational systems and to identify areas for improvement, examination, and emulation. Although PISA scores and analyses alone do not offer insights into the causal nature of relationships between educational inputs and outputs, the test has nevertheless stimulated a broad range of analytic work that has driven macro-educational policymaking, system-level change, and school reform within the participating countries. These analyses suggest that public accountability and peer pressure associated with PISA have played a significant role in shaping public policy (Schleicher, 2009, 2010).

This chapter examines the merits of PISA comparisons as drivers for educational change. International comparisons like PISA can put national goals into a global perspective, identify different approaches to existing practices and policies, measure educational progress, and apply pressure on the political processes to realize educational change (Schleicher, 2009, 2010).

Putting National Goals Into a Broader Perspective

International comparisons can put national performance into a broader perspective (Schleicher, 2009, 2010). Countries can analyze their standings

Note: This chapter is based on Schleicher, A. (2009). International assessments of student learning outcomes. In L. M. Pinkus (Ed.), *Meaningful measurement: The role of assessments in improving high school education in the twenty-first century* (pp. 95–118). Washington, DC: Alliance for Excellent Education; Schleicher, A. (2010). International comparisons of student learning outcomes. In A. Hargreaves, A. Lieberman, & M. Fullan (Eds.), *Second international handbook of educational change* (pp. 485–504). New York: Springer.

on PISA against educational systems or regions in similar contexts and set national goals on how to improve and reach the next level of performance.

In Brazil, the country's education minister has frequently cited the PISA-benchmarked Basic Education Development Index (IDEB), created in 2005, as key to improving school results across the country, and more specifically, to reach the average PISA score by 2021 (Schleicher, 2009). IDEB is a national assessment for 4th, 8th, and 11th grades in Portuguese and mathematics. IDEB is customized for each school but is also aligned with PISA (OECD, 2010b). As opposed to holding all schools accountable to the same performance goal, IDEB instead affords schools an opportunity to track their own performance over time. The Education Ministry hopes that IDEB will highlight areas for improvement and help schools pay more attention to student-level data in core subject areas (OECD, 2011).

Seeing What Can Be Achieved in Education

The impact of international comparisons is naturally largest when the comparisons reveal that a country's education system performs comparatively poorly or when it performs differently from how educational performance is publicly perceived (Schleicher, 2010). In Germany, the 2000 PISA results revealed large performance disparities across socioeconomic lines, suggesting that students from more privileged backgrounds had access to higher-quality educational institutions (Schleicher, 2009). This revelation countered the public perception of the educational system. The public outcry rallied policymakers to invest in early childhood education, in the creation of national educational standards, and in the development of an infrastructure to better support students from disadvantaged backgrounds and underserved communities (Schleicher, 2009). A decade later, results from PISA show important improvements in Germany, both in terms of quality and equity of educational outcomes (OECD, 2010a). Germany illustrates an example of how an education problem can be illuminated by an international comparison test and elevated to a public policy sphere, motivating key stakeholders into immediate action that can swiftly change existing educational practices.

Measuring Educational Improvement

International comparisons can help nations assess their educational progress over time (Schleicher, 2009, 2010). Although PISA has shown that many countries are successfully raising educational performance, the pace of change across nations has greatly varied (Schleicher, 2010). South Korea ranked 24th on educational output two generations ago. Today, due to progressive educational change and national investments in the education system, the country is one of top PISA performers, and 98% of young adults graduate successfully from upper secondary education (OECD, 2012). Poland offers another promising example. Poland has over the last decade focused on turning around low-performing schools and reducing variable quality across schools, both of which led to significant student learning gains. Positive progress can be attributed to strategies such as the development of a new national assessment system, national standards, a core curriculum, and greater school autonomy (Loveless, 2012).

Influencing the Political Process of Reform

International comparisons can inform the political process and influence reform policies (Schleicher, 2009, 2010). In Mexico, the 2007 national education survey found that a majority of parents believed that their children received high-quality education and attended good schools (De Cossio & Bagur, 2007). Yet, the 2006 PISA scores identified that half of the country's 15-year-olds performed at or below the lowest performance levels set by the international assessment (OECD, 2007). Although schools have significantly improved from the previous generations, the lack of public will to drastically reform schools diminishes the role that education policy plays in Mexican public discourse (Schleicher, 2009). To mitigate this issue, the Mexican government has included PISA targets into its educational goals and created incentives for schools and training for teachers in order to improve instructional practices and strengthen the core learning standards for all students (OECD, 2010b).

International Comparisons as a Powerful Reform Instrument

International comparisons can be a powerful instrument for policy reform and transformational change. Particularly in today's interdependent world, where individuals work with and interact with people from across the globe, creating educational systems that support 21st-century learning is essential. Paying attention to a nation's educational performance and comparing it to higher-performing countries can have an impact on intended, implemented, and achieved policies and practices in a given nation (Schleicher, 2010). Although caution is needed when making direct comparisons, given the context-specific nuances of individual education systems, PISA shows that international comparisons can be a powerful instrument for inviting social and educational reforms that would better serve students in the short and long term (Schleicher, 2009).

References

De Cossio, R. D., & Bagur, A. R. (2007). *Mexican national survey to parents regarding the quality of basic education.* [*Primera encuesta de opinión de los padres de familia sobre la educación en México*]. Mexico City, Mexico: Instituto de Ingeniería de la UNAM [Institute of Engineering at UNAM]. Available at www.sep.gob.mx/es/sep1/sep1_Bol2501007

Loveless, T. (2012). *How well are American students learning?* Washington, DC: The Brookings Institution.

Organisation for Economic Co-operation and Development. (2007). *PISA 2006 science competencies for tomorrow's world.* Paris: Author. Available at www.oecd.org/pisa/pisaproducts/pisa2006/pisa2006results.htm

Organisation for Economic Co-operation and Development. (2010a). *PISA 2009 results: What students know and can do.* Paris: Author. Available at www.oecd.org/pisa/pisaproducts/48852548.pdf

Organisation for Economic Co-operation and Development. (2010b). *Strong performers and successful reformers in education: Lessons from PISA for the United States.* Paris: Author. Available at www.oecd.org/pisa/46623978.pdf

Organisation for Economic Co-operation and Development. (2011, Fall). Class performance. *OECD Observer, No. 287.* Available at www.oecdobserver.org/news/fullstory.php/aid/3744/Class_performance__.html

Organisation for Economic Co-operation and Development. (2012). *Education at a glance–OECD indicators 2012.* Paris: Author.

Schleicher, A. (2009). International assessments of student learning outcomes. In L. M. Pinkus (Ed.), *Meaningful measurement: The role of assessments in improving high school education in the twenty-first century* (pp. 95–118). Washington, DC: Alliance for Excellent Education. Available at www.all4ed.org/files/MeaningfulMeasurement.pdf

Schleicher, A. (2010). International comparisons of student learning outcomes. In A. Hargreaves, A. Lieberman, & M. Fullan (Eds.), *Second international handbook of educational change* (pp. 485–504). New York: Springer.

CHAPTER 2

Teleporting Change

The Dynamics and Distortions of International Benchmarking

Andy Hargreaves

If an individual or an organization wants to improve, one of the most obvious strategies is to learn from someone who is more effective. Need to improve as a teacher? Spend time watching and talking to a teacher who performs better than you. Want to improve as a school? Visit a similar school that seems to get better results. And, if you're in the doldrums as a country, then find some place that is achieving at a higher level. It can't be that hard to do, can it?

See what happens when you try to copy what a model teacher does if that teacher's personality is different from yours, or if you have not had the months to build trust and respect with a class that he or she had. Try implementing strategies from another school that has more resources, charismatic leadership, better teachers, or a different kind of community. And, try to copy a country that is mainly Lutheran when yours is secular, when its diversity is predominantly one of recent immigration while yours bears the legacy of slavery, or when it has a relatively small population but your country is bigger and more populous than some continents. Culture, history, orientation to learning, and attitude toward authority are all important considerations when trying to learn from others. The truth is that educational reform is like ripe fruit: It rarely travels well.

The Ups and Downs of Benchmarking

The process of comparing countries against one another and learning from these comparisons has become known as *international benchmarking*

Note: This chapter is based on Hargreaves, A., & Shirley, D. (2012). *The global fourth way: The quest for educational excellence.* Thousand Oaks, CA: Corwin Press.

(Hargreaves & Shirley, 2012). Benchmarking is a method to improve existing practice, not just to measure and compare it. In industrial benchmarking, businesses scrutinize their competitors not merely to copy what they do, but to learn from their practices in a deeper way that will drive their own improvement efforts (Tucker, 2009). Industrial benchmarking involves teams looking closely at their peers, and then learning together what can be adopted and adapted from what they have seen that will fit their own organization.

National and international policy organizations such as the Organization for Economic Cooperation and Development (OECD, 2011), McKinsey and colleagues (Mourshed, Chijioke, & Barber, 2010) and the U.S. National Center for Education and the Economy (Tucker, 2011) advocate for and have adopted an educational version of industrial benchmarking–international benchmarking (Hargreaves & Shirley, 2012). According to the OECD (2011), "A strong and consistent effort . . . to do disciplined international benchmarking and to incorporate the results of that benchmarking into policy and practice is a common characteristic of the highest-performing countries" (p. 254).

Unfortunately, many educational systems approach the task of improvement through strategies that distort the process of international benchmarking or deny its relevance altogether. Four such strategies are particularly prominent: bench warming, bench pressing, teleporting, and cherry picking.

Bench Warming

In sports, a benchwarmer is a substitute player who rarely plays, spending his or her time watching teammates from the sidelines. Benchwarmers do not benchmark at all. With its aversion to learning from other countries in any transparent way, the United States acts like a team that prefers to observe itself. If there are promising reforms in Kentucky or Kansas, they carry more weight than innovations in Canada. Even though tiny Singapore was the inspiration for Den Xiao Ping's restructuring of China, that has less value to American policymakers than changes that might be occurring in a U.S. state. The United States believes that it stands to learn nothing from observing others and instead makes excuses that high-performing competitors are just too different from the U.S. context to be relevant.

Bench Pressing

In the gym, bench pressing involves repeatedly lifting weights while lying horizontally on a bench. Some countries treat benchmarking not as a process of learning and inquiry but as a kind of competitive bench pressing where each nation tries to push harder and higher than its opponents (Hargreaves & Shirley, 2012). Countries strive to be at the top of the table:

the Swedes against the Norwegians, the Belgians against the Dutch, and the rest of the world against the Asians. The Programme for International Student Assessment (PISA) is used to ratchet up a sense of public and political urgency, rather than to prompt authentic inquiry (Hargreaves & Shirley, 2012).

Teleporting

The policy strategies of some high-performing countries are promoted as models for other nations to adopt. For example, designers of educational reforms in Ontario, Canada, suggest that others should adopt their own recent policies such as focusing on literacy and numeracy and high school graduation, setting system targets for improvement, driving change through all levels of the system from the center, and providing extensive support to school staff through resources and training (Levin, Glaze, & Fullan, 2008). Yet, three other Canadian provinces that are equally high performers on PISA have very different policy designs from Ontario's, so it is hard to see why one provincial strategy should be advanced over another. Similarly, fans of the Finnish system profile the policies that they prefer, such as high-status teaching and the absence of standardized testing, but give less attention to how families approach their children's learning or the role of compulsory military service in the country's culture. Singapore's minister of education emphasizes that most political visitors to its high-performing system ignore the importance of the country's distinctive culture, and the director of the country's National Institute of Education insists that it is impossible to teleport an entire system from one country to another (Hargreaves & Shirley, 2012).

Cherry Picking

Cherry picking is the act of choosing pieces of data that suit one's own political interests while ignoring other data that are inconvenient (Hargreaves & Shirley, 2012). When commentators focus on Finland, for example, they fixate on the fact that all its teachers have master's degrees (Mourshed et al., 2010). In the case of Singapore, people often emphasize its multiple career tracks for teachers, or the fact that it awards teachers performance-based pay (Tucker, 2011). These policy items are often transported to other countries without attention to the other parts of the system to which they are connected. An example is raised by the Brown Center on Education Policy at the Brookings Institution. The report described how some commentators attribute recent dramatic achievement gains made by Poland to PISA and to the country's abolition of ability tracking. However, the report explained:

Poland's 1999 education reforms were not limited to tracking. Instead, they involved a complete overhaul of the Polish school system, including decentralization of authority and greater autonomy for schools, an increase in teacher salaries, a new system of national assessment, adoption of a core curriculum and national standards, reform of teacher education at the university level, and a new system of teacher promotion. Any one of these policies—or several in combination—may have produced Poland's gains on PISA. Some may have even produced negative effects, dragging down achievement, while others offset the losses with larger gains. The point is this: no single reform can be plucked from several reforms adopted simultaneously and declared to have had the greatest positive impact. Not based on PISA data. The data do not allow it. (Loveless, 2012, pp. 28–29)

Factors That Underpin Educational Success

Benchmarking is not about copying other systems or competing with them for the sake of it. It is about learning and inquiring into the deep principles of excellence and equity that underpin many specific systems and that can be applied with flexibility and responsiveness to one's own (Hargreaves & Shirley, 2012). In our studies, Dennis Shirley and I have identified high-performing schools and school systems that relentlessly benchmark.

Singapore's educational system is constantly learning from others—sending its professionals to earn higher degrees overseas so that they can bring back what they learn, or networking with schools in other countries to exchange practices and ideas. Two top PISA performers, Finland and Alberta, have created a partnership between schools (FINAL) to adopt and adapt ideas from each other, such as placing more emphasis on extracurricular activities as the Canadians do, or giving higher status to vocational education, like the Finns (Hargreaves & Shirley, 2012).

Through our investigations into high performance in education, we have identified nine broad factors that underpin educational success: (a) pursuing an inspiring dream rather than merely racing to the top; (b) committing to education as a common public good rather than promoting independent charter schools or academies; (c) combining innovation with improvement so that education is about more than just raising achievement scores; (d) building platforms for people to initiate their own changes rather than delivering centralized reforms through pipelines of implementation; (e) pursuing prudent rather than profligate approaches to testing; (f) putting collective professional responsibility within and across schools before bureaucratic intervention and accountability; (g) teaching less in order to learn more; (h) reforming teacher unions instead of replacing them; and (i) integrating technology with good pedagogy so that each enhances the other (Hargreaves & Shirley, 2012).

How can countries like the United States start to develop a better learning mindset? Learning from others can start out very close to home. States can halve the budgets for their centralized intervention teams and distribute the resources to schools, so that schools can help one another across district boundaries. The federal government could award 1,000 small travel grants per year for teachers and principals to visit or intern with schools during the long summer vacation in a high-performing country in the southern hemisphere like Australia or a developing country in Africa, and bring back inspiration and innovation to their own settings. Teach for America could be encouraged to partner with teacher union leaders in order to increase rates of teacher retention as a shared responsibility. If we want our children to learn, our schools must learn. And, if we want our schools to learn, our nations must be prepared to learn as well. In educational reform, this is not the time to circle the wagons, but to widen the circles of learning and influence where the world grows stronger by how its people learn to improve together.

References

Hargreaves, A., & Shirley, D. (2012). *The global fourth way: The quest for educational excellence.* Thousand Oaks, CA: Corwin Press.

Levin, B., Glaze, A., & Fullan, M. (2008). Results without rancor or ranking: Ontario's success story. *Phi Delta Kappan, 90*(4), 273–280.

Loveless, T. (2012). *How well are American students learning?* Washington, DC: The Brookings Institution.

Mourshed, M., Chijioke, C., & Barber, M. (2010). *How the world's most improved school systems keep getting better.* New York: McKinsey & Company. Available at www.mckinseyonsociety.com/how-the-worlds-most-improved-school-systems-keep-getting-better/

Organisation for Economic Co-operation and Development. (2011). *Strong performers and successful reformers in education: Lessons from PISA for the United States.* Paris: Author.

Tucker, M. S. (2009). Industrial benchmarking: A research method for education. In A. Hargreaves & M. Fullan (Eds.), *Change wars* (pp. 97–116). Bloomington, IN: Solution Tree.

Tucker, M. S. (2011). *Standing on the shoulders of giants: An American agenda for education reform.* Washington, DC: National Center on Education and the Economy.

CHAPTER 3

Directions of Change
Why the United States and China Are Moving in Opposite Directions

Yong Zhao

Like many countries in the world, China and the United States have in recent years embarked on a journey to drastically change their education system for the betterment of children. What is perplexing is that the educational changes the two countries are attempting are moving in the opposite directions–China has been making its education system more American, while America has been "de-Americanizing" its system in an effort to make it more Chinese (Zhao, 2009a). Why do the world's two largest and most powerful nations, which often see each other as rivals in many domains, have so much mutual admiration of each other's education system that they want to make a complete switch? Why are they so eager to move away from their own educational traditions, which are diametrically opposed, and follow the lead of their opponent?

Recent American Education Reforms

Education reform efforts in the United States over the last few decades have been moving toward centralization, standardization, and reliance on testing. From *A Nation at Risk* (National Commission on Excellence in Education, 1983) in the 1980s to the standards movement in the 1990s to the No Child Left Behind Act (NCLB) of 2001, and finally, to the Common Core State Standards Initiative currently being implemented, these sweeping efforts have transformed American education. The majority, if not the entirety, of American school systems have moved away from the old tradition. No longer is American education a decentralized system comprised of tens of thousands of locally controlled school districts with tremendous autonomy over

Note: The chapter is based on Zhao, Y. (2009). *Catching up or leading the way: American education in the age of globalization.* Alexandria, VA: Association for Supervision and Curriculum Development.

curriculum, instruction, and assessment. It has become a system more like that present in China before that country began its own reforms in the 1990s.

Three elements in particular have moved the U.S. system over the past decade to resemble pre-2000s China. First, NCLB was a pivotal point in American education, ushering in standardized tests as *the* measure of student knowledge, similar to Chinese practices. Second, the federal government has increased control over curriculum decisions, just like in China, requiring that all states develop rigorous curriculum standards in mathematics, reading, and science. The Common Core is further centralizing American education by imposing stipulations on the Race to the Top federal grant program requiring eligible states to adopt common curriculum standards and agree to common assessments. As a result, 45 states and three territories have adopted the Common Core. By 2014, U.S. states will have standardized tests and a Common Core curriculum, completing the country's journey to become the new China. Third, similarly to China, the implementation of NCLB has led to a significant narrowing of the public education curriculum to meet the demands of standardized tests, leading to increased instructional time on test subjects and decreased school focus on untested areas (McMurrer, 2007; Zastrow & Janc, 2004).

The American Dream: China's Education Reforms

While the United States was busy becoming China, China was hard at work becoming more American. About the time when NCLB was designed, the highest governing bodies of China (the Central Committee of the Chinese Communist Party and the State Council) issued the *Decision to Further Educational Systemic Reform and Promote Quality-Oriented Education* (Zhonggong Zhongyan [Central Committee of the Chinese Communist Party] & Guowuyuan [State Council], 1999). This landmark framework took the completely opposite direction from NCLB on three major issues: the role of testing in education, centralized authority over curriculum and assessment, and the content of the curriculum (Zhao, 2009a). The *Decision* drastically lowered the significance of testing in education by abolishing middle school entrance exams and encouraging schools to develop their own graduation exams. It granted significant authority over curriculum and testing to provincial governments and schools. The *Decision* also ended the central government's monopoly on writing and publishing textbooks.

In July 2010, around the time that America rolled out the Common Core and the Race to the Top, China released the *State Guidelines for Medium-to-Long-Term Education Reform and Development Plan* (Zhonggong Zhongyang [Central Committee of the Chinese Communist Party] & Guowuyuan [State Council], 2010). The *Guidelines* articulate major strategic goals and reform measures for Chinese education between 2010 and 2020. The *Guidelines* put tremendous emphasis on improving the overall quality of education through an increased government investment in education, universal access to early childhood and high school education, and development of world-class universities. And, to improve the quality of education, the *Guidelines* reiterate policies to reduce the stakes of testing on students, teachers, and schools, and also reduce student academic burden, broaden the curriculum, and increase school autonomy.

In many ways, China is working to emulate traditional American education, although the government may not openly or explicitly acknowledge this. The essence of the reforms is to minimize the significance of standardized testing, to grant schools and teachers more autonomy, and to encourage more innovation in provinces and local schools.

Directions of Change: Who Got It Right?

The directions may be opposite, but the goals are similar. Both China and the United States want an excellent education for their citizens. The difference in strategies comes as a result of different definitions of educational excellence and the practical problems they face. Behind these apparently contradictory movements in education reform is seemingly logical reasoning.

For the United States, the movement toward standardization, testing, and centralization is considered a logical action to close the achievement gap, the cause of which, as reform proponents argue, is a difference in what is taught in schools, teacher expectations, and teaching quality. By imposing a common standard through testing and holding schools and teachers accountable for improving the test scores, these school reformers believe that this kind of system will produce equal education quality for all children.

China, on the other hand, sees a different set of problems. Having already had a uniform national curriculum, high-stakes testing, and centralized government control of schools for a long time, it has not seen the kind of talents it desires and needs in order to transition from an economy once built on abundant and cheap labor to one that relies on creative and entrepreneurial talents (Zhao, 2009a). As a result, China views high-stakes testing as the primary culprit in its inability to cultivate creative and entrepreneurial talent. In a 1997 policy document, the Chinese Ministry of Education condemned test-oriented education, noting that it did not meet the real needs of students because it narrowly focused on the top performers, emphasized knowledge transmission and rote memorization, and used tests as the only evaluation of student knowledge, thus neglecting the moral, social, psychological, and developmental needs of children, youth, and society (Guojia Jiaowei [National Education Commission], 1997).

China's education reform should be a lesson to the United States. It is a perfect example of why common standards and high-stakes testing do not lead to equal education for all children. Tremendous gaps still exist in educational achievement across demographic lines (Tienken & Zhao, 2010; Zhao, 2009b). China is also a perfect example of the high price of standardized testing. China's stellar academic showing in international assessments comes at the cost of creativity, innovation, entrepreneurship, and student physical and emotional health (Zhao, 2009a, 2012). Unless America only wants to produce a nation of excellent test-takers, its change is moving in the wrong direction.

References

Guojia Jiaowei (National Education Commission). (1997). Guanyu dangqian jiji tuijin zhongxiaoxue shishi shuzhi jiaoyu de ruogan yijian [Several suggestions for the promotion of quality education in secondary and elementary schools]. Available at www.xhongcom.diy.myrice.com/page1/fagui/newpage8.htm

McMurrer, J. (2007). *Choices, changes, and challenges: Curriculum and instruction in the NCLB era.* Washington, DC: Center on Education Policy.

National Commission on Excellence in Education. (1983). *A nation at risk: The imperative for educational reform.* Washington, DC: National Commission on Education Excellence.

Tienken, C. H., & Zhao, Y. (2010). Common Core national curriculum standards: More questions . . . and answers. *AASA Journal of Scholarship and Practice, 6*(4), 3–14.

Zastrow, C. von, & Janc, H. (2004). *Academic atrophy: The condition of the liberal arts in America's public schools.* Washington, DC: Council for Basic Education.

Zhao, Y. (2009a). *Catching up or leading the way: American education in the age of globalization.* Alexandria, VA: Association for Supervision and Curriculum Development.

Zhao, Y. (2009b). Comments on the Common Core standards initiative. *AASA Journal of Scholarship and Practice, 6*(3), 46–54.

Zhao, Y. (2012). *World class learners: Educating creative and entrepreneurial students.* Thousand Oaks, CA: Corwin.

Zhonggong Zhongyan (Central Committee of the Chinese Communist Party), & Guowuyuan (State Council). (1999). Guanyu shenhua jiaoyu tizhi gaige quanmian tuijin suzhi jiaoyu de jueding [Decision to further educational systemic reform and promote quality-oriented education]. Available at www.chinapop.gov.cn/flfg/xgflfg/t20040326_30741.html

Zhonggong Zhongyan (Central Committee of the Chinese Communist Party), & Guowuyuan (State Council). (2010). Guojia zhongchangqi jiaoyu gaige he fazhan guihua gangyao [State guidelines for medium-to-long-term education reform and development plan]. Available at www.gov.cn/jrzg/2010-07/29/content_1667143.htm

CHAPTER 4

Mindful Teaching with Technology
Steps Toward Harmonization

Dennis Shirley

Once promoted as a cure-all for the myriad problems that educators confront, technology has lost its innocence and novelty. Educators have repeatedly found that despite elaborate promises and sophisticated sales pitches, the fundamental problems of teaching and learning persist, regardless of the new technological tools such as laptops, iPads, and cell phones. The pressing question at the current time is no longer about how rapidly new technologies can be infused in schools. Rather, we are at a historical moment that calls for greater mindful deliberation about the purposes we hope to achieve with new technologies in the first place. We can no longer accept that the sheer availability or popularity of new technologies means that they are, *eo ipso*, legitimate for learning purposes. Instead, we must probe more rigorously into the ways that new technologies can promote the best kinds of learning and cognition and can do so in ways that will sustain our young people across their life spans, rather than for an episodic, if scintillating, nanosecond.

An important dimension of our challenge is that technological change has been so rapid in recent years that it is difficult to know how to even think about it before it has metamorphosed yet again. In the past half-century, technology in schools has undergone several stages of change. According to Larry Cuban (1986), during the 1950s and 1960s, "television was hurled at teachers" (p. 36) by reformers captivated by its ability to provide or supplement lessons with entertaining content. Educators tended to resist the reformers' exhortations, fearing that they undermined the relational aspects of education (Hargreaves & Shirley, 2012).

In the 1970s and 1980s, computer laboratories gradually found their ways into schools, often with simple and mechanistic programming tasks that were rarely coordinated with a school's preexisting curriculum (Means, 2008). Physically isolated approaches to technology that were disconnected from any other dimensions of education reinforced the iconoclastic and

Note: This chapter appeared originally in Hargreaves, A., & Shirley, D. (2012). *The global fourth way: The quest for educational excellence.* Thousand Oaks, CA: Corwin Press. The chapter has been modified for inclusion in this volume, and is reprinted by permission of the publisher.

impervious character of new technology in schools. With the rise of the standards and accountability movements, technology was further marginalized as a weak curriculum area, not to be compared to the more high-stakes outcomes attached to literacy and mathematics.

Since the 1990s many curricular barriers to technology have fallen. Technology has been infused throughout the curriculum as iPads, laptops, and cell phones have become ubiquitous in the broader culture and in schools as well (Hargreaves & Shirley, 2012). This explosion of new easy-to-use devices provides educators with a plethora of opportunities to enhance student learning. However, in the vast majority of cases, computers are being used to assist with the rapid retrieval of facts, rather than developing independent skills for critical thinking and analysis (Reich, Murnane, & Willett, 2012).

Even with all of these changes, some patterns persist. Educators have found that new technologies are more difficult to master than anticipated, and that such tools can distract students from mastering the academic curriculum. While there have been some exceptions, the net result has been inconsistency and incoherence across the profession. One teacher can use Twitter as a way of rapidly gathering student feedback on a question, but still shun presentation tools like PowerPoint because they often impede meaningful dialogue and exchange. Another can have students watch Khan Academy videos as homework, but never actually use technology in class, preferring to capitalize on face-to-face tutorial relationships. Another teacher could avoid new technologies altogether. There is little consistency within schools or even within departments in the same school.

This proliferation of approaches fits well into a definition of teaching as an artisanal craft that enables its practitioners to tinker with the curriculum over the course of many years of instruction. Political philosopher Zygmunt Bauman (2007) argues that we now live in "liquid times" in which all forms of modern life are unstable. If this is so, teaching may be a consummately "liquid" profession, one that allows its practitioners to try out and revise many pedagogical approaches throughout their professional lifespans.

If teaching does indeed have this "liquid" capacity, it should be possible for educators to try out many different responses to new technologies. Andy Hargreaves and I (2012) have argued that educators can (a) *endorse* technology, (b) *question* technology, (c) *shelter* children from technology, or (d) *harmonize* technology with other interests. These orientations may exist in fruitful combination with one another in the course not only of a teacher's life span, but even within the conduct of a single class.

Endorse Technology

Many advocates of educational change can be described as "endorsers" who are exhilarated about the potential of new technologies in schools. In one recent survey, 77% of American teachers viewed the impact of digital technologies on students' research skills as mostly positive (Purcell et al., 2012). Young people in the United States spend more than twice the international average amount of time spent in school each year using media to communicate with their social networks, to listen to music or to watch videos, or for entertainment. The same platforms that provide entertainment often can also provide students with a more personalized approach to information than traditional schools have ever been able to sustain.

Endorsing new technology can lead to educational transformations that extend beyond simple access to the general curriculum. Yong Zhao (2012) provides examples of entrepreneurial activities launched by high school students with the assistance of technology that help less-developed countries to develop small businesses and protect the environment. In these cases, students are contributing to the economic and ecological vitality and sustainability of their communities.

Question Technology

While there are many praiseworthy attributes of new technologies, those who excessively endorse the infusion of digital technologies into schools may be neglectful of their distracting and addictive nature. A Common Sense Media survey (2012) found that 71% of U.S. teachers believe that their students' use of new media hurts their academic performance. While 63% of teachers agreed that the Internet helped their students to find information quickly, 71% worried that students find it increasingly difficult to keep their attention focused on solving problems where the answer is not immediately evident and some degree of persistence through frustration is necessary.

While we are finding gains in some subject matter areas for specific students, in general, expectation for rising results in the wake of technological investments have been disappointing (Hargreaves & Shirley, 2012). States such as Maine or Texas, which have spent millions on new laptop initiatives and have carefully studied their impacts, have had mixed results (Hargreaves & Shirley, 2012). Some scores in some subject areas have gone up, but others have declined, and still others have essentially remained the same (Shapley, Sheehan, Maloney, & Caranikas-Walker, 2009; Silvernail & Gritter, 2007). An anticipated revolution in learning did not occur. Similar results were found from the One Laptop per Child program that distributed 40,000 computers across 500 schools in Peru that served poor rural communities (Cristia, Ibarrarán, Cueto, Santiago, & Severín, 2012).

Such findings have strengthened the convictions of those who believe that technology cannot replace high-quality teachers, carefully selected curricula, and finely honed assessments. Resisters argue that other factors, more powerful than technological tools, appear to be determinative in shaping academic outcomes.

Shelter Children from Technology

A third group goes further than those that question new technologies. They believe their responsibility is to *shelter* young people from technology (Hargreaves & Shirley, 2012). This group finds that the extraordinary amount of time now spent with new media is competing with the time that they have available for physical exercise, learning to play a musical instrument, or developing skill with the visual arts. In their view, children need to be shielded from technological influences, which reshape neural pathways in a number of ways that have negative social consequences. These include a lessening of empathy, which is developed through reading facial reactions and other forms of body language; an expectation of immediate responses and impatience with delayed reactions; and lack of perseverance in overcoming complex and ambiguous problem sets (Small & Vorgan, 2008).

Harmonize with Technology

If educators enact diverse orientations towards technology, such as endorsing it, questioning it, and sheltering students from it, how can these different standpoints be harmonized so that students are not constantly being jolted from one vantage point to another? Ngee Ann Secondary School in Singapore provides an example of harmonizing with technology. Located in a multiethnic, multilingual, and working-class sector of the city, Ngee Ann has endorsed technology by creating new learning platforms for self-directed learning (Hargreaves & Shirley, 2012). The school emphasizes social entrepreneurship in service to others. Ngee Ann students have joined students in other Southeast Asian nations in order to promote greater environmental awareness in their communities. Ngee Ann students and faculty utilize social media and diverse design tools to enhance communication and deepen learning for important social and environmental goals, an approach that has won them numerous awards (see www.ngeeannsec.moe.edu.sg).

While Ngee Ann deserves its reputation as a technology innovator, interviews with faculty revealed that traditional instruction continues to play a significant role, as students do not spend more than 20% to 30% of their learning time utilizing new technologies. Tutorial relationships, small-group work, and new technologies are blended skillfully and continuously with one another, with an emphasis on improving consistent student learning across the diverse forms of instruction, curriculum, and assessment (Hargreaves & Shirley, 2012).

Ngee Ann Secondary School shows us that mindful teaching with new technology is not a distant utopia, but a lived reality. This harmonization of the old and the new reveals just how resilient and inventive educators can be as they work to explore new technologies with their students. Beyond endorsing technology, questioning it, or sheltering students from it, there lies a rich and abundant new *terra incognita* of educational change that harmonizes the best of traditional practices with the promise and potential of technology. (For more information about mindful teaching, see MacDonald & Shirley, 2009, or go to www.mindfulteacher.com).

References

Bauman, Z. (2007). *Liquid times.* Malden, MA: Polity.

Common Sense Media. (2012). *Children, teens, and entertainment media: The view from the classroom.* San Francisco: Author.

Cristia, J. P., Ibarrarán, P., Cueto, S., Santiago, A., & Severín, E. (2012). *Technology and child development: Evidence from the one laptop per child program.* Washington, DC: Inter-American Development Bank.

Cuban, L. (1986). *Teachers and machines: The classroom use of technology since 1920.* New York: Teachers College Press.

Hargreaves, A., & Shirley, D. (2012). *The global fourth way: The quest for educational excellence.* Thousand Oaks, CA: Corwin.

MacDonald, E., & Shirley, D. (2009). *The mindful teacher.* New York: Teachers College Press.

Means, B. (2008). Technology's role in curriculum. In F. M. Connelly, M. F. He, & J. Phillion (Eds.), *Sage handbook of curriculum and instruction* (pp. 123–144). Thousand Oaks, CA: Sage.

Purcell, K., et al. (2012). How teens do research in the digital world. *Pew Research Center.* Available at www.pewinternet.org/~/media/Files/Reports/2012/PIP_TeacherSurveyReportWithMethodology110112.pdf

Reich, J., Murnane, R., & Willett, J. (2012). The state of Wiki usage in U.S. K–12 schools: Leveraging Web 2.0 data warehouses to assess quality and equity in online learning environments. *Educational Researcher, 41*(1), 7–15.

Shapley, K., Sheehan, D., Maloney, C., & Caranikas-Walker, F. (2009). *Evaluation of the Texas technology immersion pilot: Final outcomes for a four-year study (2004–05 to 2007–08).* Austin: Texas Center for Educational Research. Available at www.tcer.org/research/etxtip/documents/y4_etxtip_fin al.pdf

Silvernail, D. L., & Gritter, A. K. (2007). Maine's middle school laptop program: Creating better writers. Available at www.k12blueprint.com/sites/default/files/Impact_on_S tudent_Writing_Brief.pdf

Small, G., & Vorgan, G. (2008). *iBrain: Surviving the technological alteration of the modern mind.* New York: HarperCollins.

Zhao, Y. (2012). *World class learners: Educating creative and entrepreneurial students.* Thousand Oaks, CA: Corwin.

CHAPTER 5

From the Periphery to the Center
Broadening the Educational Change Discourse

Helen Janc Malone

The U.S. education reform narrative has over the last decade centered on global competition, labor market demands, standardized tests, achievement gaps, and common standards. Standardized tests, in particular, have been used in education policy to highlight problem areas in students' basic content knowledge, to draw attention to the disparities in test performance across demographic lines, and to raise awareness about the general shortcomings of our existing schooling system. However, the current education policy focus on externally driven, top-down reforms is myopic. This chapter argues that there are four lines of inquiry that should be moved from the periphery to the center of the public educational change discourse: (a) broadening discussions about the purposes of education beyond labor market arguments, (b) focusing on student-centered learning, (c) recognizing the role outside-of-school learning plays in supporting student education, and (d) engaging front-line stakeholders—teachers, students, families, and community members—in leading educational change efforts.

Education Beyond Global Marketplace Needs

The increasingly knowledge-based economies have put a premium on 21st-century skills, defined as core academic subjects, life and career skills, learning and innovation skills, and information, media, and technology skills (Partnership for 21st Century Skills, 2012). In his book *The Global Achievement Gap*, Tony Wagner (2008) argues that the U.S. education system must adapt to meet the demands of the global market, and calls for a wider adaptation of 21st-century skills acquisition in our schools. Complementary to such skill demands are broader educational goals that promote citizens' positive integration into civil society.

Globalization has made the world interconnected and interdependent. The proliferation of technological tools and their applications have been a "knight's move," a transformational change in how we interact and connect to one another and the world (Haste, 2007). Living in a pluralistic global society requires an "intellective competence" (Gordon, 2006), an ability to engage in a multicultural society, to comprehend in a nuanced way the historical, sociocultural, and geopolitical factors that guide the lives of others. Such knowledge can be acquired through an engagement in civil society, which entails civics education, community and public service, and an understanding of democratic principles that many nations aim to preserve or to which they at least aspire. Singapore, as illustrated in Chapter 23 of this book, offers a promising vision of how a country can embrace a broader educational philosophy and lead to positive whole-system change.

Student-Centered Education

For some students in low-performing U.S. schools, education consists of rote memorization in preparation for standardized tests. As Yong Zhao (2009) warns, although such a practice might create a faction of great test-takers, this educational style is not conducive to the 21st-century demands that both the public and private sectors decry are needed. What instead produces authentic learning is an integrative approach that actively connects classrooms with real-world applications.

Learning requires mutual participation by students and teachers. Students need to feel a sense of agency, motivation, and relevance of curricular content to their lives (Zhao, 2011). For students to feel engaged in their own learning, versus being passive bystanders, they need to have choices and control in their learning (Smith, 2006; see also Cámara, Chapter 10 of this book). In the United States, innovative delivery models of instruction such as High Tech High, Rocketship, and Hive Learning Network offer students opportunities to engage in applied learning, utilizing technology, teamwork, and project-based learning to set their own pathways to reaching academic goals (Davidson & Goldberg, 2009). High Tech High, for instance, provides students with personalized instruction; engages them in peer learning, community service, and internships; and assesses students' knowledge through performance-based learning (see www.hightechhigh.org).

Authentic learning also requires "mindful teaching" (Hargreaves & Shirley, 2009). As addressed in Part II of this book, effective instructional practices are nurtured primarily through professional efforts that emphasize continuous improvement and refinement, collective inquiry, critical problem analysis, and innovative solution generation.

Learning Outside the Classroom

Students across the globe generally spend a fraction of their daily time in schools; however, they continue to learn throughout the day. They engage in the surrounding environment in a variety of ways: trips to museums, book clubs at local libraries, play time with peers in parks, volunteering at community organizations, or acquiring life skills at home. Nonformal and informal spaces are conduits to student learning that can reinforce and supplement the school day (Blyth & LaCroix-Dalluhn, 2011).

High-quality nonformal school- or community-based programs are important aspects of students' education and development (Eccles & Gootman, 2002; Vandell, Shumow, & Posner, 2005). In the U.S. context, such programs involve extracurricular activities, tutoring, internships, and apprenticeships across diverse disciplines. If our collective global goal is to get students ready to succeed in a society that thrives on innovation, flexibility, adaptability, and ingenuity, then we have to recognize the role that nonformal service providers play in students' active learning and engage them as partners in education reform decisionmaking.

Engaging Front-Line Stakeholders

Education policy tends to center on the institution of school as the primary unit of change (Harris & Chrispeels, 2008). School reform is often perceived by the front-line stakeholders—teachers, students, families, and community members—as something done *to* them rather than something co-constructed *with* them. Reformers seldom involve front-line stakeholders in the educational change process, generally through auxiliary teacher advisory groups, token student board members, or symbolic school events that bring families and community members together. Not only does that affect the contextual adaptation of external policies but it also stifles innovation from within schools and communities.

What creates meaningful educational change is a balance between top-down and bottom-up practices, whereby frontline stakeholder voices are integrated at all levels of decisionmaking, thus connecting classroom realities with education policies. Finland (see Chapter 24), for instance, actively involves its teaching force in curriculum development, in instructional innovations, and in education policy construction.

Students ought to be critical partners in educational decisions, as they are the most directly impacted by national and local measures (Hargreaves

& Shirley, 2009). An active youth voice that informs and acts as an equal collaborator in educational improvement efforts can assist in creating greater alignment between students' needs and that of macro-environments (Zeldin, 2004). Finally, family and community involvement cannot be left to occasional school functions (Henderson, Mapp, Johnson, & Davies, 2007), but rather, efforts should be made on behalf of those instituting educational changes to offer spaces where families and community members can bring forth ideas and strategies that shape students' learning environments.

Why Broadening the Conversation Is Necessary

International benchmarking, standardized tests, and school reform policies matter, but so do the voices of those who are directly impacted by them. Motivating learners implies a broader consideration of factors. Although some students might be highly engaged in their schooling by the notion that passing a test can get them a stable job after graduation, others require a different spark, hands-on learning, room for creativity, and a sense of belonging in a community and the broader society. Similarly, if we want to improve the quality of education, we must foster reflective teaching practices and collegial collaboratives that offer spaces for ongoing development, refinement, problem-solving, and innovation, as well as room for family and community engagement. If we are serious about creating meaningful educational change, we must engage voices that are often left on the periphery of system-wide reform.

References

Blyth, D. A., & LaCroix-Dalluhn, L. (2011, Fall). Expanded learning time and opportunities: Key principles, driving perspectives, and major challenges. In H. J. Malone (Ed.), *New directions for youth development: Expanded learning time and opportunities, No. 131* (pp. 15–27). San Francisco: Jossey-Bass.

Davidson, C. N., & Goldberg D. T. (2009). *The future of learning institutions in a digital age.* Cambridge, MA: The MIT Press.

Eccles, J. S., & Gootman, J. A. (Eds.). (2002). *Community programs to promote youth development.* Washington, DC: National Academy Press, National Research Council and Institute of Medicine, Committee on Community-Level Programs for Youth.

Gordon, E. W. (2006). Intellective competence: The universal currency in technologically advanced societies. In E. W. Gordon & B. L. Bridglall (Eds.), *Affirmative development: Cultivating academic ability* (pp. 3–16). New York: Rowman & Littlefield.

Hargreaves, A., & Shirley, D. (2009). *The fourth way: The inspiring future for educational change.* Thousand Oaks, CA: Corwin.

Harris, A., & Chrispeels, J. (Eds.). (2008). *International perspectives on school improvement.* London: Routledge.

Haste, H. (2007). Good thinking: The creative and competent mind. In A. Craft, H. Gardner, & G. Claxton (Eds.), *Creativity wisdom and trusteeship* (pp. 96–104). Thousand Oaks, CA: Corwin.

Henderson, A. T., Mapp, K. L., Johnson, V. R., & Davies, D. (2007). *Beyond the bake sale: The essential guide to family-school partnerships*. New York: The New Press.

Partnership for 21st Century Skills. (2012). Framework for 21st century learning. Available at www.p21.org/overview

Smith, M. (2006, November 15). The old and the new: A learning revolution. Paper presented to the Asian Pacific Society, Beijing, China.

Vandell, D. L., Shumow, L., & Posner, J. (2005). After-school programs for low-income children: Differences in program quality. In J. Mahoney, J. Eccles, & R. Larson (Eds.), *Organized activities as contexts for development: Extracurricular activities, after-school and community programs* (pp. 437–456). Mahwah, NJ: Erlbaum.

Wagner, T. (2008). *The global achievement gap.* New York: Basic Books.

Zeldin, S. (2004). Youth as agents of adult and community development: Mapping the processes and outcomes of youth engaged in organizational governance. *Applied Developmental Science, 8*(4), 75–90.

Zhao, Y. (2009). *Catching up or leading the way: American education in the age of globalization.* Alexandria, VA: Association for Supervision and Curriculum Development.

Zhao, Y. (2011, February). Students as change partners: A proposal for educational change in the age of globalization. *Journal of Educational Change, 12,* 267–279.

PART II

IMPROVING PRACTICE

Capacity building through collective inquiry and shared leadership has been promoted through a burgeoning body of research as a promising way to build deep instructional practices and improve teaching. Educators are increasingly stepping out of their classrooms to collaborate and engage in daily practices that promote continuous improvement. From school-based practices to professional development programs, it is evident that what builds capacity are spaces where teachers feel open to share, learn, challenge, fail, innovate, and succeed both individually and collectively. Although the accountability era promotes data-centered habits, practices that inspire teachers are those that go beyond student achievement test scores and focus on pedagogy and instructional practices that enrich teachers and students alike. This Part illustrates evidence-based practices that promote high-quality teaching and learning.

Louise Stoll opens this Part with Chapter 6, "Capacity for Learning: Getting Serious About Practice Improvement." She draws attention to the need to move away from status quo approaches to teaching and to focus on collective inquiry and innovations as anchors of good practice. Stoll calls on school leaders to create interlinking systems for practice improvement that value creative thinking, innovation, and diverse instructional approaches, environments where teachers can collectively engage in capacity building and development. Such systems, she proposes, can help balance teacher learning and accountability and assist in building self-improving school systems.

James P. Spillane approaches instructional practice from a distributed perspective. In Chapter 7, "Diagnosing and Designing for Schoolhouse Practice: Educational Administration and Instructional Improvement," Spillane argues that prepackaged school reforms do not align well with individual school needs because they fail to account for the local context. Instead, he offers a different approach to school reform and instruction—engagement by school leaders, principals and teachers, in diagnostic and design work as a means to define goals, identify strategies for improvement, and address problems.

Stephen E. Anderson, in Chapter 8, "The Enduring Challenge of Achieving Effective Teaching on a Large Scale," focuses on two approaches to system-wide improvement of instructional practice, the implementation and the professional learning community (PLC) approaches. He evaluates the implementation approach, which requires that teachers be trained in specific instructional interventions, and he raises concerns about the approach's ability to improve quality of instruction. He juxtaposes the implementation approach with the PLC approach, suggesting that system-wide change is more likely attained through PLC, due to its inherent design to support collegial learning and development.

Ann Lieberman furthers the discourse on teacher improvement by offering models that are shaping professional development of teachers and instilling collective inquiry. In Chapter 9, "Ways of Knowing: Developing Teacher Knowledge in the 21st Century," Lieberman presents three examples of promising national teacher training models–The National Writing Project (NWP), The New Teacher Center (NTC), and the Teacher Learning and Leadership Program (TLLP)–that build a sense of peer community and collaboration as vehicles for capacity-building within the teaching profession. She concludes that when teachers are involved in the design of their own professional development, it helps create a collegial community and alter the school culture toward teachers.

This Part closes with an example of an innovative approach to capacity building and quality practice, presented by Gabriel Cámara in Chapter 10, "The Small Origins of a Large-Scale School Reform in Mexico." Cámara traces the development and growth of the tutorial relationships model of teaching and learning from poor rural classrooms in Mexico to a nation-wide middle grades strategy for public education. He addresses the benefits of training teachers and students to serve as content-based mentors, and the power this strategy has to empower teachers and to help students own their learning trajectories.

Collectively, the chapters argue that what promotes quality teaching are system-wide environments that offer teachers ownership of their own development and learning and that create a culture comprised of professional collaboration, innovation, and empowerment of practitioners to lead educational change from within the classrooms.

CHAPTER 6

Capacity for Learning
Getting Serious About Practice Improvement

Louise Stoll

Let's face it: Improving practice is extremely hard. It is easy to find research or guidelines on how to improve schools, yet what comes across as straightforward when you read or hear about it is altogether different as you try to introduce it, move it from one person or place to another, or ensure its sustainability. The landscape is littered with examples of educators who engage enthusiastically in improvement efforts that ultimately make little difference. Improving practice, especially in fast-changing times, does not just mean getting better at doing the same thing; it means that practice must also become more innovative. Improvement is also an increasingly high-stakes accountability business in many countries. In England, my own country, evolving policy changes have moved responsibility down to the front line in what is intended to be a self-improving school system (Department of Education, 2010). To rise successfully to that kind of challenge means that educators have to keep learning, unlearning, and relearning (Stoll, Fink, & Earl, 2002).

Capacity for Learning

Capacity for learning is a qualitative, generic, and holistic concept. It allows individuals to learn from their environment and to apply that learning to new and changing situations, thereby becoming increasingly adaptive (Stoll, 2009, 2010). To create capacity means thinking about each part of the system and the interlinked and mutually reinforcing ways of improving learning.

Note: This chapter is based on Stoll, L. (2009). Capacity building for school improvement or creating capacity for learning? A changing landscape. *Journal of Educational Change, 10*(2), 115–127; Stoll, L. (2010). Connecting learning communities: Capacity building for systemic change. In A. Hargreaves, A. Lieberman, M. Fullan, & D. Hopkins (Eds.), *Second international handbook of educational change* (pp. 469–484). New York: Springer.

Evidence is mounting that collaborative inquiry and other forms of social learning have more powerful impacts on teachers' practice and student learning than individual developmental experiences (Timperley, Wilson, Barrar, & Fung, 2007). The most thoughtful professional learning communities offer a vehicle for deepening and enriching practice through joint practice development (Fielding et al., 2005), mutual exploration, co-construction of new strategies, and seeing their own practice through different lenses.

Learning is also enhanced by external expertise. Researchers play an important role in supporting educators' collaborative inquiry and injecting research findings, theoretical insights, and critical friendships that challenge current thinking. In England, Teaching Schools, professional development institutes that train teachers, develop leaders, support low-performing schools, and promote research and development, are charged with promoting and coordinating collaborative research and development across their alliance schools. In many cases, university researchers are helping them introduce and evaluate disciplined, collaborative inquiry and practice, such as school-to-school reviews and adapted forms of Japanese lesson study.

Local, state, and national leaders can support educators by modeling and participating in collaborative learning, including superintendent-led instructional rounds that lead to their own theories of action (City, Elmore, Fiarman, & Teitel, 2009), or the Austrian Leadership Academy, where school leaders–local, regional, and national policymakers–and leaders of teacher training institutions work across roles in coaching pairs and collegial learning sets to problem-solve and support each other's changing practice (Schley & Schratz, 2012).

Stimulating Learning Conversations

Educational change depends "on what teachers do and think" (Fullan, 2007, p. 129) and on what they say. Talk is at the heart of connections and activities; it needs to be purposeful, focused, nourished with evidence and ideas, an opportunity to blend people's tacit knowledge with explicit external knowledge (Nonaka & Takeuchi, 1995). Based on my evaluation of a London district learning network comprised of secondary and special schools, to make a sustainable difference in practice, teachers, middle and senior leaders, and district staff must be able to articulate what they do and why, developing and extending a shared language (Stoll, 2012). Their deep learning conversations are mutually respectful but they also challenge assumptions, create dissonance, and move thinking toward new knowledge (Earl & Timperley, 2009). Significantly, they are also focused on ensuring changes in practice.

Practicing Learning and Creativity

Schools and school systems need to be environments where teachers have the opportunity to practice their craft and develop expertise. It is vital to develop a learning orientation where learning is valued for its own sake rather than for achievement, and where teachers collectively engage in learning (Dweck, 2012). In such an environment, experimenting, tinkering, and refining practice would be valued, supported, championed, and commonplace.

Schools must be places where teachers can develop the intellectual confidence they need to explore new ideas, ask questions, and make mistakes from which they can learn (Stoll & Temperley, 2009). The conditions most conducive to nurturing teachers' creativity are in schools and systems where leaders of learning have opportunities to explore their own creativity and to encourage and promote creativity among colleagues.

Successful professional learning communities take teachers part of the way: They enable teachers to develop deep and trusting professional relationships that support them in the hard work of inquiring into their own and colleagues' practices and in working together on joint projects that demonstrate their commitment to improving their practice and their students' learning. From this secure foundation, with the right kind of leadership, a professional learning community can become a springboard for creative practice and provide an environment in which teachers' creativity can thrive. Schools like this are creative learning communities.

Creative leadership is the other important ingredient needed to design conditions conducive to teacher creativity. In the current accountability environment, teachers might worry that experimenting with practice would be risky. Leaders who value experimentation and creative thinking, who allow teachers to be exposed to diverse thinking and instructional approaches, who model creative approaches, and who believe that people learn through failure, are more likely to create a collaborative school environment and to see teachers open up to new ways of doing work.

Balancing Creative Teacher Learning and Accountability

How do we balance creative teacher learning and accountability at the school level? A school I worked with developed its own research-based learning policy, and there was a steep and powerful learning curve for all involved. However, several questions remain that are yet to be adequately addressed in practice: Is the balance between creative learning and accountability strictly a matter of school leadership and collaborative teacher culture? What is needed at district and national levels to allow space for creative adult learning to take place within and between schools? What changes in district, state, or national policy practice will be needed? Are there barriers that prevent such practices to take a long-term hold within schools? If so, how can they be overcome? Are we really serious about practice improvement?

References

City, E. A., Elmore, R. F., Fiarman, S. E., & Teitel, L. (2009). *Instructional rounds in education: A network approach to improving teaching and learning.* Cambridge, MA: Harvard Education Press.

Department of Education. (2010). The importance of teaching: The schools white paper. Available at www.gov.uk/government/uploads/system/uploads/attachment_data/file/175429/CM-7980.pdf

Dweck, C. S. (2012) *Mindset: How you can fulfill your potential.* New York: Constable & Robinson Limited.

Earl, L., & Timperley, H. (2009). *Professional learning conversations: Challenges in using evidence for improvement.* New York: Springer.

Fielding, M., Bragg, S., Craig, J., Cunningham, I., Eraut, M., Gillinson, S., Horne, M., Robinson, C., & Thorp, J. (2005). *Factors influencing the transfer of good practice* (Research Report RR 615). Nottingham, UK: University of Sussex and Demos.

Fullan, M. (2007). *The new meaning of educational change* (4th ed.). New York: Teachers College Press.

Nonaka, I., & Takeuchi, H. (1995). *The knowledge-creating company: How Japanese companies create the dynamics of innovation.* New York: Oxford University Press.

Schley, W., & Schratz, M. (2012). Developing leaders, building networks, changing schools through system leadership. In T. Townsend & J. MacBeath (Eds.), *International handbook of leadership for learning* (pp. 267–295). New York: Springer.

Stoll, L. (2009). Capacity building for school improvement or creating capacity for learning? A changing landscape. *Journal of Educational Change, 10*(2), 115–127.

Stoll, L. (2010). Connecting learning communities: Capacity building for systemic change. In A. Hargreaves, A. Lieberman, M. Fullan, & D. Hopkins (Eds.), *Second international handbook of educational change* (pp. 469–484). New York: Springer.

Stoll, L. (2012). Stimulating learning conversations. *Professional Development Today, 14*(4), 6–11.

Stoll, L., Fink, D., & Earl, L. (2002). *It's about learning (and it's about time).* London: Routledge.

Stoll, L., & Temperley, J. (2009). Creative leadership: A challenge of our times. *School Leadership and Management, 29*(1), 63–76.

Timperley, H., Wilson, A., Barrar, H., & Fung, I. (2007). *Teacher professional learning and development: Best evidence synthesis iteration.* Wellington: New Zealand Ministry of Education. Available at www.oecd.org/edu/school/48727127.pdf

CHAPTER 7

Diagnosing and Designing for Schoolhouse Practice

Educational Administration and Instructional Improvement

James P. Spillane

High-stakes accountability tied to student performance has contributed to a vibrant market of prepackaged school reform remedies in American education. Market supply is matched by market demand as eager consumers, practitioners, and policymakers seek solutions to ill-defined problems that fall under the umbrella of improving student performance on state-mandated tests (Spillane & Coldren, 2011). In a complex education "system" and a largely unregulated marketplace where nonsystem agencies (e.g., textbook publishers, testing agencies) increasingly thrive and are supported by government policy (Burch, 2006; Cohen, 1982), decisions about quality and fit are delegated to local schools, where quality control is mostly left to suppliers' testimonials and either weak or pseudo-science. Schools find themselves in the unenviable position of having to steer instructional improvement in this impoverished, disorganized, and unsettled terrain that we call an education system (Spillane & Coldren).

The Challenge for School Leaders

Improving student achievement will depend on improving classroom teaching, including better teacher preparation and development programs, teacher selection processes, and tenure evaluation systems. Though all these avenues are necessary, none is likely sufficient on its own. Still, one element that can make an impact on the classroom is improved school

---

Note: This chapter is inspired by the introductory chapter in Spillane, J. P., & Coldren, A. F. (2011). *Diagnosis and design for school improvement: Using a distributed perspective to lead and manage change.* New York: Teachers College Press.

administration. Syntheses and meta-analyses suggest that effective school leadership and management are critical in improving teaching (Hallinger & Heck, 1996; Leithwood, Louis, Anderson, & Wahlstrom, 2004; Robinson, Lloyd, & Rowe, 2008).

School leaders must do more than simply select a prepackaged program. Although savvy shopping is necessary, it is not sufficient for several reasons. First, school leaders have to figure out which prepackaged reforms address their school's particular problems and circumstances (Spillane & Coldren, 2011). This involves local *diagnostic* work. Second, if the challenge is improving the practice of leading and managing instruction, prepackaged reforms alone will not work because these interventions (e.g., Learning Walks, School Improvement Planning, Instructional Rounds) offer only broad scripts for practice (Spillane & Coldren). The success of a particular reform package in a particular school will ultimately depend on how its script is put into practice—*performed* on the ground. Third, prepackaged reforms offer no comprehensive coverage for all the challenges faced by school leaders and, further, one size rarely fits all so that most prepackaged reforms have to be tailored to fit local school circumstances. Thus, school leaders will have to engage in redesigning prepackaged interventions and existing infrastructural arrangements, as well as designing new ones (Spillane & Coldren).

The Work: Diagnosis and Design

Diagnosis and design are core aspects of leading and managing instruction in schools and school systems (Spillane & Coldren, 2011). A diagnosis and design orientation affords school leaders a central role in efforts to lead and manage instruction.

Diagnosis involves figuring out the nature or cause of something: What is going on here and what might account for what is going on? How and when are students dropping out of advanced mathematics classes? How is it that early elementary students are not learning to write informational pieces by the end of the 3rd grade? Diagnostic work defines goals and identifies strategies to ameliorate the defined problems. It is critical to acknowledge here that problems in schools are not waiting around to be discovered by school leaders or the external consultants and policymakers on whom they often rely for such matters. More important, data do not define problems on their own (Spillane & Miele, 2007); people do!

Design involves shaping aspects of the situation in purposeful ways to address particular goals. School leaders work at molding their organizational infrastructure elements for particular purposes and organizational functions. This organizational infrastructure includes formal organizational routines (e.g., faculty meetings, teacher evaluations, walkthroughs), formal positions (e.g., coach, mentor teacher), and tools (e.g., classroom observation protocols, meeting agendas). School leaders must design and redesign these aspects to address certain functions. Research suggests that schools design organizational routines to address various challenges, such as tailoring professional development to teacher needs, providing regular feedback to teachers on student performance, engaging teachers in instructional leadership work, motivating and supporting teachers' instruction in writing, and standardizing teacher grading practices (Spillane & Diamond, 2007).

Few are well prepared for either the tasks of diagnosis or design. School leadership preparation programs do not cultivate such a mindset. Of course, diagnosis and design are never as straightforward or simple in practice as they appear in theory. Nevertheless, prepackaged remedies can play an important role in improving schools, but they must be carefully selected and wisely tailored to local institutional and organizational circumstances.

Framing Diagnosis and Design: A Distributed Perspective

Diagnosis and design require a conceptual or analytical framework to guide and focus the work. Such frameworks are often left implicit in research and development and making them explicit is necessary to ensure that the work is efficacious. Absent such frameworks, practitioners, policymakers, and researchers are simply talking past one another as they grapple with leading and managing instruction.

I argue for a distributed perspective. It differs from the dominant perspective that privileges the thoughts and actions of the individual school leader (e.g., mentor teacher, teacher leader, principal) by equating the practice of leadership with the behaviors of those individuals, mainly the school principal (Spillane & Coldren, 2011). Framing leadership and management from a distributed perspective involves, at least, two conditions. First, it is an acknowledgment that leading and managing instruction may involve more than the person at the top of the organization—the school principal (Spillane & Coldren). Other formally designated school leaders, such as mentor teachers, coaches, and assistant principals, may play a key role in leading and managing instruction. Informal leaders may have an additional hand in the work of leading and managing instruction (Spillane & Coldren).

Second, and most important, when taking a distributed perspective, leadership and management practice is an essential focus. A distributed perspective frames this practice in terms of people's interactions with one another rather than just the actions of a single individual. Thus, the interactions among school leaders and teachers along with other internal and external school stakeholders (e.g., students, parents, teachers, district policymakers, local community members) are essential to understanding leadership and management practice (Spillane & Coldren, 2011). Social norms, organizational routines, formal positions, and rules enable and constrain everyday interactions in schools. Thus, the situation is a defining aspect of everyday leadership and management practice. If patterned human interactions as enabled and constrained by the situation are the essence of the practice, then, we have to accept that emergence and improvisation are unavoidable properties of practice.

We cannot design practice; we can design *for* practice. We design *for* practice by examining (diagnosis) how elements (e.g., organizational routines, formal positions) of our situation enable and constrain interactions and then, redesign these elements or design new elements to enable interactions and to transform the focus or substance of existing interactions (Spillane & Coldren, 2011).

Adopting a Diagnostic Mindset

In thinking about the practice of leading and managing instruction, we must get beyond individual actions—equating practice with the actions of the school principal or some other formal leader, and acknowledging that practice takes shape in social interactions. Organizational routines (e.g., grade-level meetings, school improvement planning), tools (e.g., student assessment instruments, teacher observation protocols), and other aspects of the situation frame and focus the interactions among school staff (Spillane & Miele, 2007). As a result, it is stretched over individuals as enabled and constrained by aspects of their situation. Such a conceptualization poses a tougher challenge when it comes to improving practice than if we simply thought about practice as improving what the school principal says or does.

As state and federal government agencies impose on local schools high-stakes accountability mechanisms tied to student achievement on standardized tests, school staff are left to figure out how best to improve classroom teaching and learning. And they have to do so quickly while barraged with a clutter of prepackaged reform remedies from the education sector. It is tempting under such circumstances to rely on implementing prepackaged remedies. Although such a strategy may be necessary for instructional reform, it is unlikely to be sufficient. Adopting a diagnostic mindset toward the practice of leading and managing instruction so as to design for the improvement of that practice is essential.

References

Burch, P. (2006). The new educational privatization: Educational contracting and high stakes accountability. *Teachers College Record, 108*(12), 2582–2610.

Cohen, D. K. (1982). Policy and organization: The impact of state and federal educational policy on school governance. *Harvard Educational Review, 52*(4), 474–499.

Hallinger, P., & Heck, R. H. (1996). Reassessing the principal's role in school effectiveness: A review of empirical research, 1980–1995. *Educational Administration Quarterly, 32*(1), 5–44.

Leithwood, K., Louis, K. S., Anderson, S., & Wahlstrom, K. (2004). *How leadership influences student learning: A review of research for the Learning from Leadership Project.* New York: The Wallace Foundation.

Robinson, V. M. J., Lloyd, C. A., & Rowe, K. J. (2008). The impact of leadership on student outcomes: An analysis of the differential effects of leadership types. *Educational Administration Quarterly, 44*(5), 635–674.

Spillane, J. P., & Coldren, A. F. (2011). *Diagnosis and design for school improvement: Using a distributed perspective to lead and manage change.* New York: Teachers College Press.

Spillane, J. P., & Diamond, J. B. (2007). *Distributed leadership in practice.* New York: Teachers College Press.

Spillane, J. P., & Miele, D. B. (2007). Evidence in practice: A framing of the terrain. *Yearbook of the National Society for the Study of Education, 106*(1), 46–73.

CHAPTER 8

The Enduring Challenge of Achieving Effective Teaching on a Large Scale

Stephen E. Anderson

If the quality of teaching is known to be the most significant in-school factor affecting student achievement, then it is amazing how little is known about how to improve the quality of teaching at a system level, despite half a century of research on teacher and school effectiveness and change. This chapter discusses two approaches to system-wide improvement in instructional practice: the program or practice implementation approach and the professional learning community approach.

The Implementation Approach to System-Wide Instructional Improvement

The implementation approach to instructional improvement requires the designation of specific instructional interventions (e.g., learning materials, teaching methods, assessment tools) as desirable, and setting up a support system to train and assist teachers to incorporate them into the teaching and learning process. This approach can be used with particular instructional programs or with freestanding instructional practices that teachers select and apply independent of a specific program.

One of the persistent issues with the implementation approach is clarity about expected teacher actions. Bennett and Rolheiser (2001) propose a framework for classifying instructional practices in terms of their specificity: instructional concepts, organizers, strategies, tactics, and skills. Instructional concepts are the big ideas that convey teachers' pedagogical beliefs, such as making learning relevant or personalized, but they have to be converted into specific pedagogical actions. Instructional organizers provide frameworks for planning organized sets of teaching and learning activities, and are often research-supported, but also have to be transformed into concrete teaching and learning activities. Classic examples would be the seven-step lesson design model for direct instruction (Hunter, 1994) and the theory of multiple intelligences (Gardner, 1993). Instructional strategies consist of multistep pedagogical actions, often based on research, such as the jigsaw method of cooperative learning and concept mapping. Jigsaw, for example, is a small-group learning strategy in which each of the teammates within a cooperative group becomes an expert on different aspects of one topic of study, after which the members of the group teach one another about their area of expertise. Students do a culminating task to demonstrate their learning across all aspects of the major topic. Tactics are less complex actions, and less well supported by research on their contribution to learning, such as Think-Pair-Share, Four Corners, and other simple group-learning activities (e.g., Gibbs, 1995; Kagan, 1994). In Four Corners, for instance, the teacher posts different dimensions of a topic in designated corners of the room. Students select a particular dimension in response to a question, and move to that corner, where they pair up to discuss the reasons for their choice. The teacher then selects pairs from each corner to share their thinking with the class. Instructional skills refer to proficiency in the enactment of things such as providing clear instructions, posing effective questions, or managing classroom behavior.

The implementation approach to developing teachers' expertise on a wide scale is highly dependent upon professional development strategies employed at the system level with successive instructional innovations. This is difficult and costly to do without violating what is known about effective staff development and support for teacher learning (Joyce & Showers, 1980; Loucks-Horsley, Harding, Arbuckle, Murray, Dubea, & Williams, 1987). We know that introducing teachers to instructional programs and practices through one-shot workshops or off-site courses without follow-up assistance in the classroom setting is unlikely to lead to more than superficial implementation. We know that train-the-trainer models of professional development are useful for disseminating basic knowledge about new programs and practices, but often fall short of enabling the effective transfer of training into the classroom, partly because the trainers may have little experience implementing the innovations, and partly because of inadequate follow-up.

Some basic concerns with the implementation approach to improving the quality of instruction include: (a) uncertainty that the programs and practices promoted will actually make a significant difference in student learning; (b) variability in the specificity of instructional actions that teachers are expected to enact; (c) the quality of support for implementation; and (d) variability in teacher mastery of the instructional programs and practices adopted. Without effective ongoing support and an enabling professional culture, teachers may routinize their use of new programs and practices at suboptimal levels of mastery, thereby reducing the potentially positive effects on student learning (Anderson & Kumari, 2009). The implementation approach to improvement in instruction persists in the current push to identify and disseminate best practices, based on the belief that academically higher-performing schools must be doing something better in the classroom that would help account for their success. Actions to promote the replication of best practices, however, only reinforce the outside-in implementation approach to instructional improvement. So, what is the alternative?

The Professional Learning Community Approach to Instructional Improvement

The professional learning community (PLC) approach to instructional improvement presents a distinct alternative to the innovation implementation approach to instructional improvement. From a small-scale study of teacher collaboration, teacher learning, and student achievement in eight schools, Little (1982) first sketched out the key ideas about the practice and impact of teachers collaborating professionally. In schools where teachers routinely talked about teaching and learning, planned and problem-solved with colleagues, learned together to improve their teaching, and engaged in mutual observation and feedback, continuous staff development was a norm and student achievement was higher. Two requirements for this collegial work were an opportunity to collaborate and a genuine sense of common purpose and interdependence. Research on PLCs continued throughout the 1980s (Rosenholtz, 1989), 1990s (e.g., Fullan & Hargreaves, 1992; Louis, Marks, & Kruse, 1996), and today (Dufour, Eaker, & Dufour, 2005). A key shift in the current view of teacher collaboration is the emphasis on analyzing student assessment data and on accountability for results of instructional intervention.

Notwithstanding the professional appeal of this vision, the viability of the PLC approach to instructional improvement at the school district, state, or national level has yet to be demonstrated in North American schools. For that, we need to look internationally, and most specifically, at the model of Japanese "lesson study" as described by Stigler and Heibert (1999). In the lesson study approach, Japanese teachers working in grade, division, or special topic teams determine foci for lesson development, based on evidence of problems in student learning. The teacher teams investigate the selected problem and possible solutions, and design a lesson. Team members pilot the lesson while others observe. They debrief and refine the lesson. The process is repeated until the lesson achieves the intended results. Successful research lessons are shared across the school and with educators from other schools. Lesson study is a craft-based process of teacher inquiry and learning, supported by the school system, and built into the professional culture and work of Japanese schools and teachers. Improvement in teaching practice occurs as part of what teachers collectively do over their careers, not as an in-service event or limited to the use of a specific external program or practice. Although variants of lesson study have been introduced on a smaller scale elsewhere in the world, the policy and infrastructure supports for implementation have not been replicated at the system level.

Developing and Sustaining High-Quality Instruction

The significant issue addressed in this chapter is the enduring challenge of how to develop and sustain high-quality instruction across entire school systems among practicing teachers. The implementation approach relies on the successive introduction and teacher training to support the use of externally developed instructional programs and teaching methods. A major challenge of the implementation approach is how to create and sustain a professional development system that can lead to expert replication of promising programs and practices in multiple schools and classrooms on an ongoing basis. The professional learning community approach relies on teacher capacity and opportunity in schools to collectively analyze student learning needs, to create or select instructional interventions to address those needs, to implement the interventions, and to evaluate the results on an iterative basis. Instructional improvement is embedded in teachers' routine work at the school level.

Creating and sustaining professional working conditions and teachers' capacity to engage in collective work and incremental improvement in instructional practices system-wide remains a challenge (Hargreaves & Fullan, 2012). Although presented as alternatives, the two approaches are not incompatible. Teacher access to external knowledge about promising teaching practices can be a vital source of ideas to supplement teachers' creative ideas. However, deep expertise that leads to wide-scale quality instruction is only likely to be achieved through sustained institutionally supported teacher collaboration in genuine PLCs in schools, regardless of the source of ideas.

References

Anderson, S., & Kumari, R. (2009). Continuous improvement in schools: Understanding the practice. *International Journal of Educational Development, 29*(3), 281–292.

Bennett, B., & Rolheiser, C. (2001). *Beyond Monet: The artful science of instructional integration.* Toronto, Ontario, Canada: Bookation Inc.

Dufour, R., Eaker, R., & Dufour, R. (Eds.). (2005). *On common ground: The power of professional learning communities.* Bloomington, IN: Solution Tree.

Fullan, M., & Hargreaves, A. (1992). *What's worth fighting for? Working together for your school.* Toronto: Ontario Public School Teachers Federation.

Gardner, H. (1993). *Multiple intelligences: The theory in practice.* New York: Basic Books.

Gibbs, J. (1995). *Tribes: A new way of learning and being together.* Sausalito, CA: CenterSource Systems.

Hargreaves, A., & Fullan, M. (2012). *Professional capital: Transforming teaching in every school.* New York: Teachers College Press.

Hunter, M. (1994). *Enhancing teaching.* New York: Macmillan College.

Joyce, B., & Showers, B. (1980). Improving inservice training: The messages of research. *Educational Leadership 37,* 379–385.

Kagan, S. (1994). *Cooperative learning.* San Juan Capistrano, CA: Kagan Cooperative Learning.

Little, J. W. (1982). Norms of collegiality and experimentation: Workplace conditions of school success. *American Educational Research Journal, 19*(3), 325–340.

Loucks-Horsley, S., Harding, C., Arbuckle, M., Murray, L., Dubea, C., & Williams, M. (1987). *Continuing to learn: A guidebook for teacher development.* Andover, MA: Regional Laboratory for Educational Improvement of the Northeast and Islands & National Staff Development Council.

Louis, K. S., Marks, H., & Kruse, S. (1996). Teachers professional community in restructuring schools. *American Educational Research Journal, 33*(4), 757–798.

Rosenholtz, S. (1989). *Teachers' workplace: The social organization of schools.* White Plains, NY: Longman.

Stigler, J., & Heibert, J. (1999). *The teaching gap: Best ideas from the world's teachers for improving education in the classroom.* New York: Free Press.

CHAPTER 9

Ways of Knowing

Developing Teacher Knowledge in the 21st Century

Ann Lieberman

U.S. educators, policymakers, and researchers have for years struggled with how to improve teaching and have sounded the alarm about the lack of quality professional development opportunities within the teaching profession. Professional development has been maligned by teachers as yet another quick hit, as scores of outside developers have sought to come to schools and districts, most often without the necessary conditions and supports for teachers to actually incorporate new ideas into practice.

Extensive research and careful examination of teacher learning practices has now identified several examples of what conditions are needed to support teacher learning over time. Within the education field, three programs in particular–The National Writing Project (NWP), The New Teacher Center (NTC), and the Teacher Learning and Leadership Program (TLLP)–are considered illustrative of the best practices. Extensive evidence shows that NWP leads to more classroom writing and that NTC leads to greater retention of mentored teachers. In TLLP, there is collaboration between the policymakers and the practitioners, and research is currently under way to evaluate three cohorts of teachers.

The National Writing Project

The National Writing Project (NWP) was started over 30 years ago as a literacy-oriented teacher learning community. The program consists of a partnership between a college or a university and a group of teachers in a given location. There are now 198 NWP sites in the United States (see http://www.nwp.org).

From 1998 to 2000, a colleague and I studied two NWP sites, Los Angeles and Oklahoma, after we heard from many teachers that the writing project is like "magic" (Lieberman & Wood, 2003, p. 14). Both of us sat through the summer institutes of our respective sites documenting what we saw. We found that teachers came to the summer institutes expecting to be *told* how to better teach writing, but became involved in a set of social practices that not only taught them how to think differently about writing, but also engaged them as the primary learners in the process (Lieberman & Wood, 2003). Teachers wrote, got feedback, and revised their work. Teachers taught their peers their best lessons or strategies, and teachers read literature and research and discussed it among themselves. No one ever told the teachers what to do or how to learn. Little by little, teachers went public with their work, and learned how to give critical feedback to their peers and participate in a community (Lieberman & Wood, 2003). We wondered as researchers if any of the activities in which they were participating would appear when we went to visit their classrooms. What we witnessed in both sites were practices that represented the NWP's model for teacher learning (Lieberman & Wood, 2002):

- Approaching every colleague as a potentially valuable contributor.
- Encouraging teachers to teach other teachers.
- Creating public forums for sharing, dialog, and critique.
- Turning ownership of learning over to learners.
- Situating learning in practice and relationships as well as relevant knowledge.
- Providing multiple entry points into learning communities.
- Thinking about teaching through reflection on learning.
- Sharing leadership.
- Adopting an inquiry stance.
- Rethinking professional identity and linking it to professional community. (p. 298)

These social practices were integrated into the summer institute. The institute started with what teachers knew and moved to reading research and literature, and listening to the expertise of other teachers who had been in the summer institute in previous years (Lieberman & Wood, 2002). Teachers learned to build a professional community by engaging in making their teaching public, by learning how to give constructive feedback, and by working together to improve their practice (Lieberman & Wood, 2002, 2003; Lieberman & Friedrich, 2010).

The New Teacher Center

The New Teacher Center (NTC) began over 14 years ago when the idea of the induction years became an important topic in California. The NTC hallmark was to mentor beginning teachers in a way that students could learn regardless of their background and that mentors could become teacher leaders, deepening the teaching profession as they worked with new teachers. Today, the NTC touches educators in 35 states and four different countries. There are more than 7,500 mentors working under the banner of the NTC (see http://www.newteachercenter.org).

The NTC model is adopted by districts, which invite an NTC delegation to work with a number of outstanding teachers who take on the job of part-time mentors for a year. Each mentor has from five to ten novice teachers, often in different schools. Mentors come together in a weekly forum to discuss their problems and their own learning.

A number of research studies have documented teacher retention, showing that NTC mentoring matters significantly and that those who get mentored stay in teaching beyond the first 3 years (Kapadia, Coca, & Easton, 2007). Other research centered on the mentor-mentee relationships and has deepened our understanding of the complexities of the mentoring role and the different tensions that abound working in diverse school contexts (Lieberman, Hanson, & Gless, 2012). The NTC model hopes to accomplish a deeper understanding of the problems of novice teachers as well as how to continue to document the mentor-mentee relationship and what brings about successful mentoring.

Teacher Learning and Leadership

From 2005 to 2007, the Ontario Minister of Education called together a working party to discuss with the Ontario Teachers Federation (OTF) and several ministers what would be most effective professional learning for teachers. One key decision was that professional development should be self-selected, attentive to adult learning styles, goal-oriented, sustainable over time, and built on evidence-based research as well as formal and informal data (Lieberman, 2010). *Choice* for teachers was a centerpiece of the program, as was *coherence* describing the connection between the educational needs set by the Ministry, board (district), or school (Lieberman). These recommendations became the Teacher Learning and Leadership Program (TLLP).

A short application was designed for teachers to apply to work individually or with a team to organize and engage in professional development over a year's time. The applications asked teachers how their projects would benefit professional development of colleagues, student learning, and individual teachers (Lieberman, 2010). Budgets ranged from $1,000 to $10,000, with additional funding for project expansion (Lieberman).

The TLLP program helps teachers launch promising practices. Preliminary themes from a research study showed that there is an enormous array of subject areas, including special projects such as boys' learning, technology, and issues of community involvement. Teachers have created materials that have been disseminated widely and have engaged in communities of practice. Zoe Brannigan-Pipe, for instance, has introduced Livescribe, an active online teacher community.

What We Have Learned So Far

All three of these illustrated programs have led to positive changes in teachers' learning and leadership. Both the NWP and the NTC are operating on a national scale. The actual practice of teachers advancing their learning while working on their own teaching appears to have produced powerful adult learning models. After a certain amount of practice, researchers, as well as teachers, know what questions to ask, what problems they have, and how well they and their students are progressing. In each of these examples, we also begin to see the kinds of organizational conditions that help teachers engage in collaborations and communities with their peers. In the NWP, teachers become a community during the summer institute and learn from their peers. They realize that this is what they can do in their classrooms. In the NTC, novice teachers learn by starting with their own problems in the classroom and being mentored to deal with them. In the NWP and the TLLP, teachers learn how to improve their practice by organizing ways of dealing with teaching problems with their peers.

These three programs teach us that when teachers are heavily involved in designing their own learning with their peers, it helps build a community of peers who learn together and, in so doing, changes the professional culture of the school. All three examples could and should change the national discourse and policies that enable teacher learning. All three of these programs respect teachers and the complicated job they do. All three start with what teachers know first. This may be the real key to educational change. We could start there!

References

Kapadia, K., Coca, V., & Easton, J. Q. (2007). *Keeping new teachers: A first look at the influences of induction in the Chicago Public Schools.* Chicago: University of Chicago, Consortium on Chicago School Research.

Lieberman, A. (2010, June). Teachers, learners, leaders: Joining practice, policy and research. *Educational Leadership, 67.* Available at www.ascd.org/publications/educational-leadership/summer10/vol67/num09/Teachers,-Learners,-Leaders.aspx

Lieberman, A., & Friedrich, L. D. (Eds.). (2010). *How teachers become leaders: Learning from practice and research.* New York: Teachers College Press.

Lieberman, A., Hanson, S., & Gless, J. (2012). *Mentoring teachers: Navigating the real-world tensions.* San Francisco: Jossey-Bass.

Lieberman, A., & Wood, D. (2002). Untangling the threads: Networks, community and teacher learning in the National Writing Project. *Teachers and Teaching: Theory and Practice, 8*(3), 295–302.

Lieberman, A., & Wood, D. (2003). *Inside the National Writing Project: Connecting network learning and classroom teaching.* New York: Teachers College Press.

CHAPTER 10

The Small Origins of Large-Scale School Reform in Mexico

Gabriel Cámara

The rapid multiplication of tutorial networks in Mexican public schools, from 2004 to the present, did not originate in the well-thought-out plan of a newly appointed administration, as has usually been the case with large-scale educational changes. Instead, the networks began forming at the very bottom of the educational system, in eight poor rural schools. The results in those schools soon demonstrated to neighboring towns and, eventually, to policymakers, the power that tutorial relationships have both to develop genuine interest among teachers and students and to generate conditions for productive learning inside classrooms.

Positive results and support from a highly centralized system of public education have made tutorial relationships a flagship of educational reform. Today, tutorial relationships are mandatory for all school teachers (across approximately 222,000 preschool, 571,000 elementary, and 381,000 middle schools), as part of their Basic Training Course (Secretaría de Educación Pública [Ministry of Education], 2011).

Since 2009, the 9,000 schools with the lowest academic achievement on the national standard test are being helped by tutorial networks linked through state and regional nodes of trained teachers who periodically visit the schools and work collegially with teachers and students. During summer 2012, all 1st-year mathematics and language teachers in the country's 37,000 middle schools were personally trained in basic elementary school content in order to help them train their students to act as mentors for their classmates so that no one in the group would be left out when it came to receiving personal attention and assistance. Making room for tutorial relationships in all middle schools has made time on-task and content a function of the students' mode of learning, not the other way around. Ongoing official projects to improve middle schools, to redefine the role of technical advisors in the system, and to integrate centers of school supervision are being inspired by the achievements of tutorial networks.

A Tested Approach to Better Learning

Introducing tutorial relationships in ordinary classrooms was a last-resort attempt to foster interest in learning in disenfranchised communities of teachers, students, and parents, in some of the country's poorest rural towns. An important testing ground, prior to 2004, were the 360 Post-primary Centers run by the National Council for the Promotion of Education. There, the impersonality of classrooms (the commonly hypothesized reason for the pervasive lack of interest among teachers and students in basic education) could be tested in settings where most other variables were controlled: all instructors were young, temporary, and nonunion; few students, though very different from one another in age and disposition; very uneven daily attendance at school due to competing survival commitments; and an inequality of resources such as mentors.

The then director of the Council gave promoters free rein to design and operate the Post-primary Centers with the sole goal of effectively improving learning. Impersonality was countered by tutorial relationships that could only be obtained if the instructor demonstrated a clear academic capacity and students were genuinely interested in acquiring academic competency. Practically, this meant going beyond particular subject matter and learning autonomously from written texts.

Training instructors to learn to dialogue with different stakeholders meant that they had to prepare lists of mastered subjects that they could offer to students. The students, in turn, could freely choose among the subjects offered. The commitment was to establish a tutorial dialogue, and persevere in the endeavor until both the student and the instructor were satisfied with the results. Then, by reflecting on the learning process, the students were ready to present that process in public and, very importantly, to improve their mastery and continue learning as they became effective tutors to fellow students. This way, a learning community was formed in which every member was able to teach and learn with interest.

Making Education Personal

The primary effect of training teachers and students in tutorial relationships is ethical rather than academic. Apprentices feel, some of them for the first time, that they are being personally attended to, are being asked to choose what they want to learn, and are receiving help from a knowledgeable tutor whose mastery has been demonstrated. Tutoring always produces some tangible, valuable learning, and the opportunity to teach others what one has mastered becomes the privileged occasion to learn in depth.

The effect of tutoring teachers on subject matter that they have not mastered or barely know is immediate and doing so does not require elaborate or prolonged training courses. Initially, teachers would offer their students a few well-known themes (a scientific piece, a poem, a mathematics problem). The task of advisors and other teachers in the network is to constantly help increase the quantity of themes taught by teachers, who in turn, offer them to their students. Teachers and students feel the need to give others the opportunity to try a healthier, more productive way to relate in school. Within the confines of the school world, they have created the equivalent of a social movement whose strength rests on the enthusiasm of individuals who have tasted the joy of learning in settings where many had before experienced frustration. The inner dynamics of change rest on the energy that is under each person's control, "the one resource that is almost equally distributed among people" (Illich, 1973, p. 12).

As the tutorial networks spread from small multigrade schools to larger schools with more students, the practice of tutorial relationships overtly counters the impersonal, compulsory school system. Students in the compulsory environment are not free to choose subjects due to rigid discipline and schedules. As higher authorities encourage schools to modify traditional practices in order to make room for tutorial relationships, teachers commonly devote extra time to tutor a few students who later multiply the practice inside the classroom. In this way, teachers cease being the only dispensers of knowledge and become organizers of a learning community, supported by advisors in a regional network who regularly visit them. Sometimes tutorial relationships substitute for standard classes. This depends on the disposition of the immediate authorities and the determination of teachers and students, and, increasingly, of parents.

The tutorial networks promote learning and positive social exchanges, even though they are increasingly taking place in a system that historically favored formal requirements over academic excellence. Tutorial networks are laying the ground for a more rigorous teaching profession, with visible worthy accomplishments, standards derived from successful collegial practice, and justly earned local prestige. The new educational design does not offer knowledge in the abstract, but rather, accommodates service to the individual's interests and personal ways of learning. Content and time thus become a function of learning, not of institutionally defined regularity. It appears that the tutorial school reform strategy will continue to gain popularity over the traditional pedagogical approaches once common in Mexican schools.

"Obedient" Decisionmaking

In 2008, the undersecretary of Basic Education, having witnessed the positive effects of tutorial relationships in a one-room middle *telesecundaria* school, decided on the spot to officially promote the practice nationally. However, the practice of tutoring is void if it is imposed on teachers, so the local authorities were offered the possibility of forming tutorial networks with the help of those that were already in existence and with the support of a group of central promoters.

It is true that political pressure to improve academic outcomes had been mounting, and that the structural changes had not produced significant results. It is also true that supporting tutorial networks in small, multigrade schools did not require great institutional changes or negotiations with the national teachers' union. When the tutorial networks were made mandatory for the 9,000 schools with the lowest average score on the national standardized tests, conditions for a productive learning environment were imposed. Freedom was still essential, however, because tutorial relationships can only take place consensually. It could be said that the policy guiding tutorial networks has been a case of "obedient" decisionmaking.

The new learning communities are showing progress. Students who once scored at the bottom on the national standardized tests are now scoring above the national average. Dropout rates are declining, and more students are graduating from middle schools and being promoted to high schools. The successful expansion of tutorial networks not only among low-performing schools but also among regular schools reveals the power of an educational approach that focuses on the interests and needs of ordinary teachers and draws on the ability of students to direct their own learning and to enable classmates to do it as well.

References

Illich, I. (1973). *Tools for conviviality.* New York: Harper and Row.

Secretaría de Educación Pública [Ministry of Education]. (2011, June). *Por el que se establece la articulación de la educación básica, No. 592* [*Agreement to establish joint basic education*]. Cuauhtémoc, México: Author. Available at www.reformapreescolar. sep.gob.mx/normatividad/acuerdos/acuerdo_592.pdf

PART III

EQUITY AND
EDUCATIONAL JUSTICE

"Education for all" and the promotion of equitable learning opportunities illustrate central goals of many societies across the globe. Fairness and inclusion are commonly cited by decisionmakers as the foremost objectives within the educational enterprise. Yet, inequalities across racial, ethnic, and socioeconomic lines persist–many low-income children and students of color attend under-resourced and/or low-performing schools. The dialogue within the education sector is often dichotomous–bifurcated between education reformers who believe that standardized assessments can assist in the identification and narrowing of the achievement gaps and those who posit that the conversation about equity in education has to move beyond student performance to directly address the underlying institutional structures (from classroom practices to educational finance) that perpetuate the historical and cultural power differentiation across demographic lines.

This Part of the book offers a critical analysis of equity and educational justice across the globe, focusing on the contextual factors that have led to the existing systems. The chapter authors propose considerations on how to approach educational justice in a way that creates system-level change and promotes equity in the learning experiences of disenfranchised students.

The Part opens with Mel Ainscow's "Equity: The Big Challenge for Education Systems" (Chapter 11). Drawing from 2 decades of research, Ainscow offers an ecology of equity framework, positing that students' educational experiences are dependent upon a range of interacting processes inside and outside the school context. He offers three factors that play a role in student learning experiences: within school, between school, and beyond school factors. He concludes that the ways to approach equity entail analyzing local circumstances, designing context-specific strategies, and collaborating with macro-initiatives to share knowledge about practices that support equity in education.

Amanda Datnow urges the field to focus on equity as the primary challenge to meaningful change in Chapter 12, "Equity-Driven Educational

Change." Borrowing from Gloria Ladson-Billings, Datnow implores education decisionmakers to move away from the "achievement gap" frame and toward the "education debt" discourse that holds institutions, rather than students, accountable for inequity. Her chapter addresses ways to mobilize research knowledge to improve educational outcomes for low-income and minority students and considers implications for policy and practice.

Sherry L. Deckman delves deeper into the discussion on educational justice by addressing ways to engage in critical diversity in Chapter 13, "Engaging Critical Diversity in Educational Reform." By posing the question of how trenchant inequity persists in the United States, Deckman explores two factors that education decisionmakers and practitioners should examine in order to create meaningful change: the current institutional system, which perpetuates power differences; and the educator silence, which leaves issues of race and inequality largely unaddressed.

Jonathan D. Jansen offers a South African perspective in Chapter 14, "The Pursuit of Excellence and Equity in Divided Countries: A South African Case." He examines the emergence of four types of schools in South Africa, and the tensions that persist pertaining to equity of access and quality of education. Jansen explores the historical, political, and sociocultural factors that have shaped the educational system and considers lessons the existing schooling structures offer about the pursuit of equity and excellence.

The Part concludes with an examination of educational justice in Latin American countries, as described by Silvina Gvirtz and Esteban Torre in Chapter 15, "Ensuring Educational Justice in Latin American Education Systems: Issues and Challenges." The authors trace the historical struggles to elevate education within the public sphere and consider the current conditions that undermine efforts to cultivate educational justice. Gvirtz and Torre look to internal efficiency and academic performance as indicators of persistent inequity and inequality in the system and call attention to the growing investments in information technology as a vehicle to educational justice by reducing the digital divide and improving access to and quality of education.

The pursuit of equity and educational justice cannot be separated from the individual countries' social, cultural, and political histories. As authors suggest in this Part, creating equitable and just learning experiences for children and adolescents entails acknowledging the institutional and societal stratifications that have systematically deprived segments of the student population of access to high-quality education. What is needed, the chapter authors argue, is an equity-driven educational change that intentionally aligns with local and national efforts that together strive to create a just society.

CHAPTER 11

Equity

The Big Challenge for Education Systems

Mel Ainscow

Throughout the world, education systems are faced with the challenge of how to achieve equity. This is most evident in the developing world, where it is estimated that almost 70 million children do not have access to basic primary education (United Nations Educational, Scientific and Cultural Organization, 2010), while in wealthier countries there remain continuing concerns regarding the way that children from economically poorer backgrounds attend the lowest-performing schools and demonstrate the worst results (Organisation for Economic Co-operation and Development, 2010). This chapter draws on research I have conducted with my colleagues over the past 2 decades mainly in the United Kingdom with the goal of determining what needs to change in order to address this crucial policy challenge.

Making Sense of Equity

In trying to make sense of the complex processes involved, it is useful to see them in relation to an "ecology of equity" (Ainscow, Dyson, Goldrick, & West, 2012). An ecology of equity refers to the role external contexts and environments–demographic, cultural, historical, and socioeconomic components–play in influencing student learning experiences inside school (Ainscow et al., 2012). It is thus necessary to address three interlinked arenas within which equity issues arise, related to: *within school factors* connected with existing policies and practices; *between school factors* that arise from the characteristics of local school systems; and *beyond school factors*, including the demographics, economics, cultures, and histories of local areas.

Note: This chapter is based on Ainscow, M. (2012, August). Moving knowledge around: Strategies for fostering equity within educational systems. *Journal of Educational Change, 13*(3), 289–310; Ainscow, M., Dyson, A., Goldrick, S., & West, M. (2012). *Developing equitable education systems.* London: Routledge.

Within School Factors

Through our research in the United Kingdom, my colleagues and I have developed an approach to school improvement that emphasizes processes of school-based inquiry (Ainscow et al., 2012). It involves the collection of diverse evidence by teams of teachers regarding groups of students perceived to be underperforming within the existing school organization. A staff team in one secondary school, for instance, explored the experiences of students they perceived to be overlooked. Observations found that teachers rarely used the names of these students. Through discussions with the students, it also emerged that they received little or no recognition for their contributions. The staff team used this information to stimulate a whole-school professional development process that focused on using practices that ensure that every student is recognized for his or her contributions and helped to make progress in learning.

Our analysis of examples such as this one led us to describe how an engagement with evidence can create "interruptions" (Ainscow et al., 2006). Under appropriate conditions, such interruptions create spaces within which teachers can work together to reconsider their practices and collaborate in experimenting with new approaches. However, we have also documented how the introduction of inquiry-based approaches can present difficulties, including finding time for it and teacher resistance to it (Ainscow et al., 2012). These difficulties point to the importance of leaders in encouraging colleagues to challenge one another's assumptions about particular students and to explore new ways of working (Ainscow et al., 2012).

Our research also draws attention to the importance of organizational cultures. It has shown that in schools that are more inclusive, organizational cultures tend to involve a respect for learner differences and a commitment among the teaching staff to finding ways of ensuring that all students participate in learning opportunities (Dyson, Howes, & Roberts, 2004). In addition, there is likely to be an emphasis on staff collaboration and joint problem-solving. Therefore, a key role for senior staff is to encourage such features within their school communities.

Between School Factors

Moving beyond what happens within individual schools, our research has thrown light on how collaboration between schools can add value to the processes of improvement and how it can help reduce the achievement gap (Ainscow & West, 2006). The Greater Manchester Challenge, a 3-year improvement project involving more than 1,100 schools, with government support of 50 million pounds, illustrates this point (Ainscow, 2012).

A detailed analysis of the local context and factors concerning students from disadvantaged backgrounds informed the Challenge. The analysis offered strategies on how to create support systems that address students' needs. Recognizing the potential of these untapped resources, it was decided that networking and collaboration would be used in order to ensure that effective practices were made available to as many students as possible.

With this in mind, Families of Schools were created. Twelve to 15 schools were grouped (via statistical modeling) on the basis of the socioeconomic backgrounds of the students. The groups connected schools that served similar communities but in different parts of the city. Engaging with data that compared the performances of schools within a Family created a sense of interruption, challenging the expectations of what is possible, encouraging sharing of expertise and collaborative efforts to explore more effective ways of reaching students who were underperforming.

Alongside the Families, more substantive partnerships were created through the Keys to Success program. Over a 3-year period, the program provided extra support for some 200 or so schools serving the most disadvantaged students. Struggling schools were matched with partner schools from another district that were known to be strong in relevant aspects (Ainscow, 2012). As a result, Greater Manchester secondary schools serving the most disadvantaged communities made three times more gains on the national examinations taken by students at age 16 than did schools across the country that did not partake in the program (Hutchings, Hollingworth, Mansaray, Rose, & Greenwood, 2012).

Within the Challenge, teaching schools were also created as another important strategy to facilitate improvement. Analogous to teaching hospitals, these successful schools provided research-based professional development programs focused on bringing about improvements in classroom practice (Ainscow, 2012). Between 2009 and 2011, more than 1,000 teachers took part in these activities. Also, 170 principals were formally designated as system leaders, taking on the task of supporting the improvement of other schools, particularly those facing challenging circumstances (Ainscow). Collectively, these improvement strategies led to positive learning gains by students in all participating schools.

Beyond School Factors

Decades of research have shown that students' learning is not only impacted by what happens inside the classroom and school, but also by demographic and environmental circumstances. The Harlem Children's Zone in New York City, for example, has illustrated that addressing student achievement is not only about high-quality teaching, but also about creating a robust system of external support that helps students access health care, afterschool programs, tutoring, college preparation, and social opportunities in ways that uplift them, their families, and their communities (Ainscow, 2012). As Dobbie and Fryer (2009) stated, The Harlem Children's Zone is "arguably the most ambitious social experiment to alleviate poverty of our time" (p. 1). For this type of partnership to take place, schools must collaborate with community partners and families to customize support for all students, whatever their personal characteristics and circumstances (Cummings, Dyson, & Todd, 2011).

Contextual analysis is needed in the efforts, such as The Harlem Children's Zone, in order to understand how local dynamics shape particular outcomes, to identify the key underlying factors at work, and to determine which factors can be acted upon and by whom. It requires that individual stakeholders understand their role and those of others within the coordinated system. For example, teachers in such an arrangement need to pay attention to students' wider needs and be able to draw on appropriate providers for support. However, such a collaboration does not necessitate that schools add more responsibility, but rather, that they share responsibility for their students with families and community partners.

Implications of Broadening Equity Strategies

Equity issues inside and outside schools need to be addressed through multidimensional strategies. Specifically, school improvement processes have to be nested within locally led efforts to make school systems more equitable. This means that the work of schools should be linked with area strategies tackling wider inequities that can ultimately connect with national policies aimed at creating a fairer society. It is a way of thinking about how educational equity can be promoted by analyzing contexts, formulating strategies that suit particular circumstances, and collaborating with others to move knowledge around (Ainscow, 2012).

References

Ainscow, M. (2012). Moving knowledge around: Strategies for fostering equity within educational systems. *Journal of Educational Change, 13*(3), 289–310.

Ainscow, M., Booth, T., Dyson, A., Farrell, P., Frankham, J., Gallannaugh, F., Howes, A., & Smith, R. (2006). *Improving schools, developing inclusion.* London: Routledge.

Ainscow, M., Dyson, A., Goldrick, S., & West, M. (2012). *Developing equitable education systems.* London: Routledge.

Ainscow, M., & West, M. (Eds.). (2006). *Improving urban schools: Leadership and collaboration.* Berkshire, UK: Open University Press.

Cummings, C., Dyson, A., & Todd, L. (2011). *Beyond the school gate: Can full service and extended schools overcome disadvantage?* London: Routledge.

Dobbie, W., & Fryer, R. G. (2009). *Are high-quality schools enough to close the achievement gap? Evidence from a bold social experiment in Harlem.* Cambridge, MA: Harvard University.

Dyson, A., Howes, A., & Roberts, B. (2004). What do we really know about inclusive schools? A systematic review of the research evidence. In D. Mitchell (Ed.), *Special educational needs and inclusive education* (pp. 280–294). London: Routledge.

Hutchings, M., Hollingworth, S., Mansaray, A., Rose, R., & Greenwood, C. (2012). *Research report DFE-RR215: Evaluation of the city challenge programme.* London: Department for Education.

Organisation for Economic Co-operation and Development. (2010). *PISA 2009 results: Overcoming social background–Equity in learning opportunities and outcomes* (Volume II). Paris: Author.

United Nations Educational, Scientific and Cultural Organization. (2010). *Education for all global monitoring report: Reaching the marginalised.* Paris: Author.

CHAPTER 12

Equity-Driven Educational Change

Amanda Datnow

The most pressing issues in educational change today are equity-related. As poverty rates grow in the United States, it is becoming increasingly difficult for students from low-income families to succeed academically. The challenges stem in large part from their lack of access to high-quality, well-resourced schools. Schools serving low-income students tend to have the greatest shortages of textbooks, the lowest numbers of qualified teachers, the fewest college preparatory programs, and are much more likely to be overcrowded and rundown.

Educational opportunities for low-income youth are further declining due to the downturn in the economy over the past several years. Since 2008, almost three-quarters of schools in California have larger class sizes, fewer counselors, and reductions in college access programs (Rogers, Bertrand, Freelon, & Fanelli, 2011). School reform efforts have been halted in many places due to the elimination of time for teaching professional development and cutbacks in teaching staff. At the same time that these school resources are being diminished, the number of youth who are struggling with homelessness, job losses among their parents, and difficulties meeting basic needs is growing. These conditions are compounded by a decrease in social welfare and health services provided by the governmental and nongovernmental agencies.

In spite of the importance of these systemic factors in shaping the educational experiences of low-income and racial minority students, most people in the field of education frame the underachievement of these students in terms of an achievement gap. Thus, reform efforts are often focused on ways to close the gap between low-income and racial minority students and their middle- and high-income White counterparts. On the contrary, Gloria Ladson-Billings (2006) urges us to consider framing the issue as an education debt. She argues that the term *achievement gap* unfairly constructs low-income and minority students as "defective and lacking" and places the burden on students to catch up. She suggests the term *education debt*, moving to a discourse that holds educators and policymakers accountable for the education resources. She further advocates for deploying our best research knowledge, skills, and expertise to alleviate the poor educational conditions and learning experiences that students receive in urban schools. So, how might we do what Ladson-Billings suggests? How might we mobilize our best research knowledge and skills to improve the educational experiences of low-income and racial minority students? I will first consider the implications for research and subsequently for policy and practice.

Implications for Research

We need more dialogue between educational change researchers and those interested in social justice. We seldom occupy the same spaces at professional conferences nor do we read the same literature. Although many educational change researchers list improved equity as an important goal of educational change, this issue may not be central to their writing. Similarly, work done in the field of social justice education sometimes does not make use of what we have learned in the field of educational change.

There are a few notable exceptions. Brahm Fleisch's (2002) study of state and school reform in South Africa illustrates how power relations around race and class influence and are influenced by educational reform efforts. Pauline Lipman's (2011) book on educational reform in Chicago provides a critical analysis of the prevailing models of educational reform, showing how the cultural politics of race and class are central to an understanding of urban school reform. Jeannie Oakes (Oakes & Rogers, 2006) and Hugh Mehan (2012) have both done decades of important work on the intersection of inequality and educational change and trained generations of their students to do the same. The work by all of these researchers straddles the fields of educational change and social justice. It is critically informed, empirically driven, and bold in its implications for equity.

Equity should be at the forefront of our research on educational change efforts. This may involve the use of different theoretical frameworks and methodologies that allow us to examine equity implications more fully. Such research may involve assembling diverse teams of researchers, or engaging local informants in the research process, not only as subjects of our work, but rather as co-constructors of the research.

Equity-focused educational change research entails stepping out of our comfort zone to have difficult conversations about race, class, and inequality in our interviews in the field. It likely involves researchers listening very carefully to *how* educators talk about the issues they are facing with respect to educating all students to high levels. Finally, it involves carefully framing our research findings so that we highlight the assets of students, families, and communities. Incorporating these kinds of changes in research on educational change may take significant effort, and constraints may exist. Although some funding agencies are eager to support equity-driven work, others do not have an equity agenda, and thus, it is then the task of the researcher to find ways to both meet the funder's goals for the research as well as to weave in a focus on equity.

Implications for Practice and Policy

Elevating an equity agenda is not just a research issue; it is also an issue of policy and practice. In the United States, federal and state accountability policies have led to the disaggregation of student achievement outcomes by racial group, English language comprehension, and/or socioeconomic status. Having access to disaggregated data has prompted educators to focus on how different groups of students are achieving in their schools. In many cases, this has led to policymakers and educators to develop educational change efforts focused on improving the educational experiences of low-income and racial minority students.

Although some of these educational reforms may indeed improve students' experiences and outcomes, in other cases such efforts may have the unintended effect of further marginalizing disenfranchised students. For example, critics of the test-based accountability movement argue that it has narrowed learning opportunities for students in urban schools, blamed teachers and students for failure on standardized tests, and has not led to capacity-building efforts that will lead to long-term school improvement (Hargreaves & Shirley, 2009).

At the local level, equity-driven change efforts continue to bump up against deep-seated beliefs about the social construction of ability, race, and class in some school contexts. Consistent with research over the past several decades, Rubin (2008) found that detracking reform in a high school serving a majority of low-income, African American, and Latino students was framed within a deficit model, thereby limiting opportunities for the very students it was meant to assist. On the contrary, in another more racially and socioeconomically diverse school she studied, educators were highly attentive to issues of equity and diversity and created personalized, flexible classroom environments that served the goals of detracking. As Rubin argued, these divergent outcomes point to how local educators' constructions of ability complicate equity-driven reform.

These findings raise some critical questions: What existing belief systems and political arrangements need to be actively addressed for the reform effort to be successful, and how might they be addressed? What in the students' past experience or circumstances might inhibit them from taking full advantage of the reform efforts? How can these be overcome? Can students' own perspectives (Yonezawa & Jones, 2009) and knowledge of the cultural communities of which they are a part (Gutierrez & Rogoff, 2003) inform the design of reform initiatives?

Mobilizing educators, policymakers, and researchers in the field of educational change to consider equity issues and work collectively may yield positive results. As the number of students growing up in poverty continues to climb and with ample room for improvement in their educational outcomes, a clear focus on equity-driven educational change is needed.

References

Fleisch, B. (2002). *Managing educational change: The state and school reform in South Africa.* Johannesburg, South Africa: Heinemann.

Gutierrez, K., & Rogoff, B. (2003). Cultural ways of learning: Individual traits or repertoires of practice. *Educational Researcher, 32*(5), 19–25.

Hargreaves, A., & Shirley, D. (2009). *The fourth way: The inspiring future for educational change.* Thousand Oaks, CA: Corwin Press.

Ladson-Billings, G. (2006). From the achievement gap to the education debt: Understanding achievement in US schools. *Educational Researcher, 35*(7), 3–12.

Lipman, P. (2011). *The new political economy of urban education.* New York: Routledge.

Mehan, H. (2012). *In the front door: Creating a college-going culture of learning.* Boulder, CO: Paradigm Publishers.

Oakes, J., & Rogers, J. (2006). *Learning power: Organizing for education and justice.* New York: Teachers College Press.

Rogers, J., Bertrand, M., Freelon, R., & Fanelli, S. (2011). *Free fall: Educational opportunities in 2011.* Los Angeles: University of California, IDEA, Los Angeles.

Rubin, B. (2008). Detracking in context: How local constructions of ability complicate equity-geared reform. *Teachers College Record, 110*(3), 646–699.

Yonezawa, S., & Jones, M. (2009). Student voices: Generating reform from the inside out. *Theory into Practice, 48*(3), 205–212.

CHAPTER 13

Engaging Critical Diversity in Educational Reform

Sherry L. Deckman

Statistics that highlight pernicious trends related to race and (under)achievement abound in conversations about educational equity and reform in the United States. We look at students' test scores broken down by race and are concerned with de facto school segregation. We decry statistics on student academic achievement, disciplinary actions, and high school completion rates that show lower-income students of color are not experiencing the same educational opportunities and success as their wealthier, White counterparts.

Yet, given all the seeming attention paid to ensuring that racially diverse students have equal educational access, how does trenchant inequity persist? An important component in answering this question relates to how educators, schools, and policymakers view and negotiate racial diversity (see Marx, 2006). This chapter explores two salient factors that leaders must actively engage in order to bring about enduring change in educational practice and policy: (a) the present structure of educational policy and institutions, which obfuscates power differences; and (b) educator silence in addressing issues of systemic inequality. I argue that meaningful change must take a critical approach to addressing issues of racial diversity.

Racializing Policy

I borrow the title of this chapter from Allison Skerrett's 2008 work, "Racializing Educational Change: Melting Pot and Mosaic Influences on Educational Policy and Practice," which calls for "approaching educational change with a racialized perspective" (p. 275). Skerrett identified four historical responses in educational policy to diversity: monoculturalism, multicultural education, antiracist education, and monocultural restoration. What she shows in her analysis is a push-pull dynamic in American education between valuing and recognizing and devaluing and ignoring the role of the country's racial diversity in schooling.

Monoculturalism, for example, which was a prevalent trend in educational policy and practice in the 1960s and 1970s, was characterized by the view that all students could achieve the same outcomes regardless of race and that "race and culture had little, if anything, to do with academic achievement" (Skerrett, 2008, p. 267). Our present era represents a return to monoculturalism with a focus on core knowledge and standards that every student should know. Antiracist education, according to Skerrett, which derives from multicultural education, never really caught on in the United States, but presents the promise of pedagogy and policy that includes a critical examination of race and equity. Although this promise exists, it remains largely unrealized.

Skerrett is not alone in suggesting that educational policy and the enactment thereof largely obscures important issues related to race and systemic inequality. Mica Pollock (2008a) calls our present time the "new civil rights era," and marks this historical moment as being characterized by a "'fragmented' system of racially unequal opportunity" (p. 11). In her work with the U.S. Department of Education's Office for Civil Rights, Pollock found addressing complaints of discriminatory treatment very difficult due to ambiguity in the law. She illustrated this ambiguity by arguing that the original intent of Title VI of the 1964 Civil Rights Act—which outlawed discrimination in federally funded programs including K–12 education to afford opportunities to people of color—was lost in recent Supreme Court decisions. Pollock argued that the Court's 2007 ruling of voluntary desegregation programs as unconstitutional (*Parents Involved in Community Schools v. Seattle School District No. 1*, 2007; see also *Meredith v. Jefferson County Board of Education*, 2006) is a blatant denial of opportunity for people of color.

Structured Inequality

Practice mimics policy in terms of its largely uncritical stance to engaging issues of racial diversity. Evidence suggests that in educational settings, even when educators believe they are acting in such a way as to value students' backgrounds and provide equal opportunity regardless of those backgrounds, they may actually be acting in ways that limit opportunity for students (Oakes, 2005; Rist, 1970). For example, Lisa Delpit (1995) focused on the "silenced dialogue" in the classroom, which refers to the unspoken power dynamic that often occurs between White teachers and students of color. Delpit recommends that teachers engage community members and explicitly instruct students about "the culture of power" in society.

When the culture of power is not made explicit, inequality may continue to be part of schools' institutional structure, as Jeannie Oakes (2005) found. In an in-depth examination of tracking in 25 U.S. secondary schools, Oakes uncovered that poor and minority students had the highest likelihood of being placed in lower tracks, which reinforced social stratification. In comparing interview quotes from students, the difference in how learning opportunities differed among lower- and high-tracked students was glaring. One high-tracked student explained what s/he had learned during a school year: "I've learned to analyze stories that I have read. I can come with an open mind and see each character's point of view . . . [the teacher] doesn't put thoughts into your head" (p. 67). Compare this response with one not atypical of the lower-tracked students in the study: "I've learned how to get a better job and how to act when at an interview filling out forms" (p. 70).

While Oakes (2005) speculated about a number of possible reasons for the disparities in what lower-tracked and higher-tracked students reported learning, she came to a clear finding: The skills higher-tracked students learn, compared with those low-tracked students learn, are valued in our society, have prestige, and permit "special access." Clearly, if we intend to make schools more equitable, we must address the root of such differences in opportunity.

Educator Silence

One reason that structured inequality may persist has to do with educators' difficulty in negotiating racial difference explicitly (Pollock, 2008a, 2008b). In fact, educators in some cases actively avoid discussing difference for a variety of reasons ranging from the fear of saying something they do not actually mean to say to concerns of being viewed as racists (Pollock, 2004; Singleton & Hays, 2008). Thus, educator conversations about race seem to fall into several patterns, in many cases avoiding, minimizing, or silencing the topic (e.g., Delpit, 1995; Singleton & Hays, 2008). What we are left with, then, may be educators who are either ignoring matters of serious consequence, or who are grappling alone, in silence, with complex or challenging issues.

Mica Pollock's (2004) research at one northern California public high school illustrates how silence ("colormuteness") exacerbates racially unequal opportunities for students at the classroom, school, and policy levels. In this case, teachers were reluctant to speak of their own roles in racial conflicts. Instead, she found educators used "de-raced" words and phrases when talking about matters of racial inequality. For example, teachers spoke of "all students," when they really meant to speak of supporting various subgroups. Pollock suggested that this same vague language showed up in school and district mission statements and reform plans. However, she argued that by not naming race we "might be making it difficult to analyze school or district inequalities that still are structured racially" (p. 222).

A concern among researchers and practitioners is that without more discussion and self-reflection, educators will not be able to meet the needs of their students from diverse backgrounds (King, 1991; Ladson-Billings, 1999). King argued that teachers who do not actively reflect upon and confront their own social position may act on "limited and distorted understanding[s] . . . about inequality and cultural diversity" in a detrimental way to their students (p. 134).

Critical Diversity as a Way Forward

When difference is uncritically explored or ignored altogether, educators can create or limit opportunities for students, even unwittingly, along race, class, and gender lines (Delpit, 1995; Ferguson, 2001; King, 1991; Ladson-Billings, 1999; Oakes, 2005). Bringing a lens of critical diversity or multiculturalism to reform-oriented policy, research, and practice may offer one opportunity for truly bringing about equity.

May and Sleeter (2010) have described this as the difference between "liberal" or "benevolent" approaches to multiculturalism and "critical" approaches. They defined liberal multiculturalism by its focus on instances of "misunderstanding differences rather than inequitable power relations" (p. 4). Across various levels of education, this approach to diversity and multiculturalism may include celebrations of cultural holidays, performances, or sharing of ethnic foods, all intended to help inform about cultural differences in a positive way. May and Sleeter noted that these feel-good ways of including multiculturalism into educational institutions can perpetuate social inequality by obscuring any analysis of unequal power structures that are "lived out in daily interactions" (p. 10). Educators who intend to bring about change must proactively ask where such power structures related to racial inequality might be invisible and bring them to the fore in any decision related to policy and pedagogy.

References

Delpit, L. (1995). *Other people's children: Cultural conflict in the classroom*. New York: The New Press.

Ferguson, A. A. (2001). *Bad boys: Public schools in the making of black masculinity*. Ann Arbor: University of Michigan Press.

King, J. (1991). Dysconscious racism: Ideology, identity, and the miseducation of teachers. *Journal of Negro Education, 60*(2), 133–146.

Ladson-Billings, G. (1999). Preparing teachers for diversity: Historical perspectives, current trends, and future directions. In L. Darling-Hammond & G. Sykes (Eds.), *Teaching as the learning profession: Handbook of policy and practice* (pp. 86–123). San Francisco: Jossey-Bass.

Marx, S. (2006). *Revealing the invisible: Confronting passive racism in teacher education.* New York: Routledge.

May, S., & Sleeter, C. E. (2010). Introduction. Critical multiculturalism: Theory and praxis. In S. May & C. E. Sleeter (Eds.), *Critical multiculturalism: Theory and praxis* (pp. 1–16). New York: Routledge.

Meredith v. Jefferson County Board of Education, 548 U.S. 938 (2006).

Oakes, J. (2005). *Keeping track: How schools structure inequality* (2nd ed.). New Haven, CT: Yale University Press.

Parents Involved in Community Schools v. Seattle School District No. 1, 551 U.S. 701 (2007).

Pollock, M. (2004). *Colormute: Race talk dilemmas in an American school.* Princeton, NJ: Princeton University Press.

Pollock, M. (2008a). *Because of race: How Americans debate harm and opportunity in our schools.* Princeton, NJ: Princeton University Press.

Pollock, M. (2008b). *Everyday antiracism: Getting real about race in school.* New York: The New Press.

Rist, R. (1970). Student social class and teacher expectations: The self-fulfilling prophecy in ghetto education. *Harvard Educational Review, 40*(3), 411–451.

Singleton, G., & Hays, C. (2008). Beginning courageous conversations about race. In M. Pollock (Ed.), *Everyday antiracism: Getting real about race in school* (pp. 18–23). New York: The New Press.

Skerrett, A. (2008). Racializing educational change: Melting pot and mosaic influences on educational policy and practice. *Journal of Educational Change, 9,* 261–280.

CHAPTER 14

The Pursuit of Excellence and Equity in Divided Countries

A South African Case

Jonathan D. Jansen

It is a question that lies at the heart of the pursuit of education justice everywhere: How does a public school make available the highest education standards to all learners while at the same time ensuring optimal access and success to the whole student body? The age-old question, of course, is often framed in terms of excellence versus equity, and in the public mind, this duality represents a choice, an inevitable tradeoff in the practice of education. Nowhere is this tension between excellence and equity more sharply felt than in South Africa, a new democracy established on the back of centuries of racial inequality first under colonialism and then apartheid. This chapter examines strategies of how schools manage, or fail to manage, the tension between equity of access and retaining the standards of education.

Race and Inequality

The well-worn narrative remains stubbornly present in post-apartheid institutions. Former White schools, in general, are better-resourced, retain better-qualified teachers, and present better academic results. Black schools generally remain under-resourced; employ teachers of variable quality; and deliver poor education outcomes, especially in the sciences and mathematics from elementary school through the end of high school. With the legal end of apartheid in the early 1990s, more and more Black students have enrolled in White schools, and these students usually experience a more stable and disciplined education, with better results, than Black students who remain inside rural and urban township schools (Jansen, 2009).

Why did the new Black government not simply take over White schools and force integration in all schools? There are many reasons: The nation founded by Nelson Mandela selected the path of reconciliation over revolutionary takeover of public institutions such as schools; the few excellent public schools accommodated the children of the Black elites and gained some legitimacy through the cover of deracialized, though often still White-dominant, middle-class learning spaces; and the real possibility of the flight of the middle classes into private education would leave a uniformly weak public sector in schooling that even in its present formation performed at the lowest ends of international tests of scholastic achievement (Jansen, 2009).

Patterns of Desegregation in Practice

In this political context—where balancing reconciliation and reparation shaped much of the post-apartheid policy landscape and where the interests of Black elites were not immaterial in decisions about how to deal with the privileged White schools—how did these race-privileged schools respond to the pressure for change? The following four school types illustrate the transition.

School A: Limited and Selective Enrollment of Black Students. In this category of schools, often White, English-speaking and urban, Black students were welcomed through the gates even before 1994—the formal end of apartheid—though in very small numbers. These public (and some private) schools, via their school governing bodies, often managed Black enrollments by insisting that students provide a proof of residence from the neighboring suburbs in order to qualify for consideration in the admissions process, that they show test scores from primary schools, and that they pay the very high school annual fees, going up to R50,000 (around $6,000). Since residential areas still strongly reflect racial divisions of the past, especially in middle-class suburbs, Black numbers would always be limited to the few in the Black elite who were able to purchase homes in the preferred areas, send their children to a White primary school, and who could afford the high tuition. The argument could be made that high standards were being maintained and the fears of Black domination could effectively be scuttled. Offering a few scholarships to a small number of poor Black students would assuage guilt and convey the message of a caring school.

School B: A Victim of White Flight. Schools serving White lower-, middle-, and working-class parents on the edges of the bigger cities pre-1990s were the most vulnerable to student attrition. As Black students came in, reaching a critical mass or tipping point, the White students gradually moved out to the neighboring White-dominant schools where they were often received empathetically (Jansen, 2009). In a short period of time, an all-White school became an all-Black school. In most cases, the White teachers left, the charge being that the new Black students were undisciplined and lacked respect for teachers. Many of these learners were expelled from township schools and were drawn to these vulnerable schools by the perception of quality education.

School C: A Racially Exclusionary School. A Type C school is a traditional urban, White Afrikaans school that uses language as the excluding element in the maintenance of racially exclusive or dominant schools. Because few Black students speak Afrikaans as their first language, the constitutional protection of language rights, in addition to the residential criteria and high tuition costs, limits Black students to very small numbers (Jansen, 2009).

In rural areas, Afrikaans schools were targeted by the Black provincial and local authorities to accommodate poor Black learners from overcrowded classrooms in the surrounding townships. Several court cases ensued in which these schools argued that enrolling Black students meant losing the Afrikaans character and language of the school, since subjects would also have to be taught in English, the preferred language of instruction among many Black learners. These schools would either lose the White students and teachers or try to maintain an uneasy balance between White and Black students.

School D: A Fully Integrated School. This school manages to retain a balance of White and Black students (with both in the 40–60% range) and in many ways represents the ideal outcomes in terms of access to high-quality education and openness to creating opportunities for Black students. Such schools achieve this racial balance because the distribution of schools in the geographic area is such that no alternative schools exist for the White students and because there is a genuine liberal attitude in the parent and teacher population where racial discrimination is not practiced; this is common in church schools and in a minority of liberal English public schools. What keeps the White students in these schools is that the teachers are almost exclusively White and the conventional high standards of education with strong disciplinary routines remain unchanged.

The Pursuit of Excellence with Equity

What do these school types teach us about the pursuit of equity and excellence? First, they demonstrate that the equity-excellence balance is an extremely difficult pursuit in a country strongly conditioned by race-thinking in the management of student enrollments and in which Whites are a minority.

Second, left unmanaged, White-minority schools would easily transition to Black exclusive schools with the loss of well-qualified teachers and strong managerial and pedagogical routines. Third, strong liberal attitudes among White parents are the most reliable guarantee of increasing Black enrollments and maintaining balanced White enrollments while making the physical and human resources of a high-quality school available to all. Fourth, government policy has limited power as an instrument in enforcing integration and maintaining quality. And fifth, only a small minority of Black students can access the small numbers of former White, privileged schools with traditions of high-quality education.

In a public education system with 29,000 schools, the question that remains is how to create schools that are excellent (high-quality education) and equitable (open to all) at the same time. Given the primacy of race in post-apartheid social and educational policies, what is now required is a political system that works actively to maintain the small percentage of good schools on a nonracial basis while simultaneously expanding the quality of education in the majority of schools. Creating such schools will require strong political intervention and renewed education strategies focused on the three key factors ruining Black schools: (a) the masses of certificated but incompetent teachers; (b) the significant losses in instructional time due to a combination of union strikes and general lethargy; (c) the slow delivery of learning materials, such as textbooks; and (d) a lack of basic infrastructure for the operation of functional schools.

At the present time, the transformation of Black schools into high-achieving schools is limited to the interventions by universities, nongovernmental organizations, and the private sector, with very positive results in pockets of excellence around the country. However, given the sheer scale of the school crisis, these interventions lack system-wide impact; for that, you need a government that can design and implement change across all public schools.

Reference

Jansen, J. D. (2009). *Knowledge in the blood: Confronting race and the Apartheid past.* Palo Alto, CA: Stanford University Press.

CHAPTER 15

Ensuring Educational Justice in Latin American Education Systems

Issues and Challenges

Silvina Gvirtz and Esteban Torre

The right to an education is recognized in Latin America as an enforceable social right (Abramovich, 2004). Specifically, educational justice means guaranteeing the right of students to access, remain in, and graduate from a school that provides high-quality education, in a context of respect for cultural diversity and without discrimination of any kind. This chapter describes the Latin American educational system in relationship to education justice, addressing the current conditions and certain aspects of the existing institutions that undermine educational justice. It concludes by identifying the challenges ahead.

The Recent History of Education in Latin America

The recent history of Latin American countries provides some clues about the current challenges to ensuring educational justice. The 1970s were marked by military governments in which the education systems were victims of a systematic plan of nullification that included the banning of books. The states drew back from educational provisions and delegated this function to individual families. The result was unequal educational performance stratified across students' socioeconomic levels (Braslavsky, 1985).

The 1980s were known in Latin America as the lost decade. The pressure exerted by the deep economic crisis had an impact on education systems: Public spending on education was increasingly seen as inefficient and uncontrolled (Braslavsky, 1999). As a result, all countries of the region reported a significant decrease in education spending, affecting crucial aspects concerning the quality and equity of education provisions (Reimers, 1991).

The revival of public interest in education in the 1990s came hand-in-hand with the search for a development model that would enable Latin American countries to participate in the globalization and technological modernization process (Braslavsky, 1999). However, the decade was also associated with an increase in social and economic inequality. In this sense, education reforms in Latin America faced the demands for productive performance and for social safety nets posed by the excluded sections of the population. The core of educational change was reduced to financial and administrative matters while undervaluing pedagogical questions. The reform policies increased student access and introduced new methods and management tools (decentralization, performance measurement, and so forth), but have not significantly altered students' learning (Tedesco, 2007).

The last decade was characterized by an improvement in economic indicators and a reduction in inequality, although the region continues to have the highest rates of social and economic inequality in the world. Improvements were supported by an active role of the state in education. Before addressing these challenges, it is necessary to discuss the current diagnosis of Latin American education systems.

Internal Efficiency and Academic Performance

Two dimensions are used as the basis for ensuring an equitable educational system: internal efficiency (enrollment, retention in grade, dropout, and graduation rates) and academic performance (as defined by the Programme for International Student Assessment [PISA] scores).

In the first decade of this century, Latin American countries experienced significant growth in net enrollment rates at all levels of education. The average enrollment rate at the preprimary level was 41.4% in 2000 and 57.7% in 2008 (United Nations Educational, Scientific and Cultural Organization [UNESCO] Institute for Statistics, 2011). Bolivia and Paraguay represent the lowest coverage, 34% and 32% respectively, while Mexico (88%), Uruguay (76%), and Argentina (71%) exhibit the highest progress. Similarly, the enrollment rate at the secondary level increased from 62.7% to 72% in 2008 (UNESCO Institute for Statistics). The lowest rate was reported by Ecuador (59%) and the highest by Chile (85%), Brazil (82%), and Argentina (80%). At primary school, the enrollment rate reached values higher than 90% in all countries of the region.

Illiteracy is still a problem in some Latin American countries. In Peru, Bolivia, and Brazil, the illiteracy rate is about 10% of the population over age 15 (SITEAL, IIPE–UNESCO, 2009). Argentina has the lowest regional illiteracy rate: 1.17%.

Grade repetition is another important internal efficiency indicator. By 2008, the average rate was 5%, while the highest reported rate was 19% in Brazil (UNESCO Institute for Statistics, 2011). However, for secondary-level education, the retention rates have not changed significantly. This is particularly worrying, considering that retention in grade is often a prelude to student dropout.

School dropout is a phenomenon that occurs at both the primary and secondary levels. By 2007, on average 14% of Latin American students dropped out of primary education (UNESCO, 2010), considering the dispersion between the highest rate (Paraguay, with 21%) and the lowest rate (Argentina, at 5%). In Argentina, research shows that a higher percentage of students (17.4%) drop out in the last 3 years of secondary school, compared with 8.4% during the first 3 years (Fundación Cimientos, 2010).

The percentage of students who graduate from secondary education is very heterogeneous (UNESCO Institute for Statistics, 2011) and is an indicator that should be observed in conjunction with the enrollment rate. Although Argentina has a low graduation rate (44%), it has one of the highest secondary education enrollment rates (80%). Looking at the reports of the Institute for Statistics of UNESCO, the most worrisome cases appear to be Paraguay and Ecuador, where low enrollment in secondary school (60% in 2009 and 59% in 2007, respectively) is combined with a low percentage of graduates (49% in 2009 and 48% in 2007, respectively).

Academic performance, defined by the countries' performance on PISA is the second key dimension of educational justice in Latin America. The PISA results offer two conclusions. The first is that countries that participate in PISA (Argentina, Brazil, Chile, Colombia, Mexico, Peru, and Uruguay) obtained below-average overall scores in reading, mathematics, and science. The second is that in 2009 the seven countries improved on their 2006 performance.

The data presented illustrate several challenges when trying to meet educational justice in Latin America. The first is to reduce illiteracy rates to zero. Another challenge is to increase the enrollment rate at the preprimary level. The evidence shows that an additional year of early education has a positive impact on the performance of students in primary and secondary levels (Galiani, Berlinski, & Gertler, 2009). It is also necessary to deepen the process of schooling in secondary schools by customizing learning to reflect cultural diversity, particularly for students who entered the education system in recent years. Any policy aimed at ensuring access to education should include a strategy that addresses major problems identified in Latin America: high grade retention and dropout rates and a low quality of student learning.

These challenges are being faced by most states in Latin America, and they are taking an active role in meeting them through educational investments, laws, and policies. In the last decade, education spending as a percentage of gross domestic product increased in most countries. The growth in net enrollment rates at all levels of education experienced by Latin American countries was in part attributed to national policy changes requiring compulsory education that favored the inclusion of disadvantaged groups, including Argentina's National Education Act (2006), Bolivia's Avelino Siñani–Elizardo Pérez Act (2010), Chile's General Act of Education (2009), Ecuador's Intercultural Education Act (2011), Uruguay's General Education Act (2008), and the Education Act in Venezuela (2009).

Social and Educational Aims of Inclusion Initiatives

Several countries in the region have started initiatives of inclusion of Information and Communication Technologies (ICT) in school through the distribution of laptops as a vehicle for promoting educational justice. These programs have at least two major aims. The social aim is to reduce the digital divide and ensure access to technology for all young people. The educational aim is to improve the quality of education and increase learning outcomes. Argentina is implementing Conectar Igualdad, a program of unprecedented magnitude in the world. By December 2012, the country had distributed 2.2 million laptops to teachers and students of public secondary schools, teacher training colleges, and special education schools. Uruguay is implementing Plan Ceibal, a policy that has completed the distribution of laptops for students and teachers of public primary schools, and it is now moving to the secondary level. Similar projects are taking place in Paraguay, Peru, Venezuela, and in some states of Brazil.

As Latin American countries continue to play an active role in creating egalitarian access to education, time and sustained policies are necessary to address trends that undermine educational justice in the region, such as high grade retention, dropout rates, and low quality of student learning. Educational justice paves the way for other actors traditionally less associated with the education system, the judiciary power and civil society organizations, to enter into the educational arena as guarantors of the right to an education. It is also essential to consider new institutional designs that can lead to the effective participation of actors that are central to the education system but who are frequently absent: parents and students. Ensuring educational justice and high-quality education for all requires a collective effort by both the governments and the society.

References

Abramovich, V. (2004). *Los derechos sociales como derechos exigibles* [*Social rights as socially enforceable*]. Madrid, Spain: Trotta.

Braslavsky, C. (1985). *La discriminación educativa en la Argentina* [*Educational discrimination in Argentina*]. Buenos Aires, Argentina: GEL–FLACSO.

Braslavsky, C. (1999). *Re-haciendo escuelas. Hacia un nuevo paradigma en la educación latinoamericana* [*Remaking schools: Towards a new paradigm in Latin American education*]. Buenos Aires, Argentina: Santillana.

Fundación Cimientos. (2010). La educación Argentina en números, No. 5 [Argentinian education in numbers]. Available at www.cimientos.org/archivos/La_educacion_argentina_en_numeros_N5.pdf

Galiani, S., Berlinski, S., & Gertler, P. (2009). The effect of pre-primary education on primary school performance. *Journal of Public Economics, 93*(1–2), 219–234.

Reimers, F. (1991). *Deuda externa y financiamiento de la educación: Su impacto en Latino-América* [*External debt and financing of education: Its impact on Latin America*]. Santiago, Chile: OREALC/UNESCO, United Nations Educational, Scientific and Cultural Organization.

SITEAL, IIPE-UNESCO. (2009). Educational Data Systems. Available at www.siteal.iipe-oei.org

Tedesco, J. C. (2007). Gobierno y dirección de los sistemas educativos en América Latina [Governance and management of education systems in Latin America]. *Revista Pensamiento Educativo* [*Educational Thought Magazine*], *40*(1), 87–102.

United Nations Educational, Scientific and Cultural Organization. (2010). *Reaching the marginalized*. EFA Global Monitoring Report. Montreal, Quebec: Author. Available at www.unesdoc.unesco.org/images/0018/001865/186524E.pdf

United Nations Educational, Scientific and Cultural Organization, Institute for Statistics. (2011). *Global education digest 2011: Comparing education statistics across the world*. Montreal, Quebec: Author. Available at www.uis.unesco.org/Library/Documents/global_education_digest_2011_en.pdf

PART IV

ACCOUNTABILITY AND ASSESSMENT SYSTEMS

The accountability era that has swept the globe has shifted education policy focus from inputs to outputs. National and international assessments are increasingly applied as tools to measure the overall success of education systems and to gauge student learning. For many countries, the emerging accountability systems mark the first time the nations have been able to visibly and comprehensively examine the state of their educational systems and the implications of the existing structures and organization on the overall student achievement. However, the increased use of external assessments has brought to the forefront the need to utilize such data as a starting point on which to build upon improvement strategies rather than to apply standardized measures as sole decision points in education policy and practice.

This Part of the book is dedicated to a critical examination of assessments and accountability systems. Its chapters pay particular attention to how the emerging accountability systems are informing the public, challenging the status quo, and reshaping education. They also draw attention to the appropriate uses of assessments and the need to create professional accountability structures that address quality in education.

The Part opens with Chapter 16, "Australian School Improvement with Transparent, Fair Comparisons," in which Barry McGaw chronicles the history and creation of the Australian national assessment system, NAPLAN, designed to offer meaningful school comparison data to inform families on the quality of their children's educational experiences. McGaw discusses how the Australian accountability system is informing practice and contends that the new assessment is a useful tool to expose problem areas and to offer data that could inspire school reform.

In Chapter 17, "Rethinking a Century-Old System: Hong Kong," Patrick Griffin discusses another critical accountability system change, that of Hong Kong, which has recently abandoned the British-based ranking system in favor of a standards-referenced accountability structure designed to recognize students' skills. Griffin underscores that by focusing attention on student learning and skill-building over fixed knowledge, Hong Kong's education system has been able to create multiple pathways to scholastic achievement and post-secondary opportunities.

In Chapter 18, "Quality Assurance System: Making Education Accountable in Russia," Elena Lenskaya describes another example of a country engaged in a significant move toward educational outputs. She offers an overview of the shift from the Soviet era inputs-driven, standardized, prescribed education system with no systemic assessments to the new outputs-centered, transparent accountability system realized through the design of a national unified exam, UNEX. Lenskaya traces the opportunities and challenges associated with UNEX and the social impact the new accountability system has had on the education sector, and foreshadows plans to create national standards and a monitoring system that would begin to address educational quality.

Madhav Chavan and Rukmini Banerji address the benefits that an assessment system can provide to capture the state of student learning across a country. In Chapter 19, "The Bottom-Up Push for Quality Education in India," the authors describe how the Annual Status of Education Report (ASER) has helped inform the public about the state of basic education across the country, particularly in traditionally underserved communities. The authors posit that what creates educational change is a demonstration of school improvement at scale that provides bottom-up pressure to reform the education system at large, one that would offer a robust accountability system focused on equity and quality of learning opportunity.

Lorna Earl closes this Part with Chapter 20, "Accountability as a Collective Professional Responsibility." She argues that the large-scale assessments are levers for policymakers but are distant from the daily practices of teaching and learning. What is needed, Earl asserts, is a focus on personal responsibility within the teaching profession and an investment in collaborative inquiry to improve student learning.

What this Part illustrates is that accountability and assessment systems matter but that they are not an end point; rather, they serve to inform the public and to aid in system design and improvement. What makes a difference in students' lives is a commitment by the entire education system to high-quality teaching and learning.

CHAPTER 16

Australian School Improvement with Transparent, Fair Comparisons

Barry McGaw

Australia has had a long history of external assessment of student achievement, with examinations at the end of elementary school and at the middle and end of secondary school. The primary use of such results was normative, serving a selection function at points of transition and possible exit. Only the end-of-secondary-school examinations remain, and they continue to play a dominant role in selection for entry to higher education. The examination results are also used in the media, quite inappropriately, to compare schools, disregarding the local contexts and demographic differences among them.

This chapter traces the introduction and development of a new assessment system during the school years, illustrates ways in which it provides school comparisons, and outlines the challenges ahead.

Development of the Current Assessment System

After years of only within-school assessments, the New South Wales state government introduced an across-school tool, the Basic Skills Testing Program in 1989 (Masters et al., 1990). The program was controversial because it provided reports to parents based on assessments that were independent of the schools; however, the tests helped reveal how the students were doing compared with others throughout the state. The other five states and the two territories soon followed, although they did not all test at the same grade level initially.

In 1996, the Ministerial Council agreed to establish national frameworks for reporting student achievement in literacy and numeracy. States and territories collaborated to relate the scales from their separate testing programs to the national frameworks; however, in the early 2000s, concerns over the adequacy of the scaling led the Ministerial Council's Performance Measurement and Reporting Taskforce to investigate and then recommend the adoption of common tests across the country. In 2007, the Ministerial Council agreed to national testing of grades 3, 5, 7, and 9, in what they named the National Assessment Program: Literacy and Numeracy (NAPLAN). The tests were developed in 2007 and used for the first time in 2008 (Australian Curriculum, Assessment and Reporting Authority [ACARA], 2008).

Making Fair Comparisons Among Schools

NAPLAN was designed to offer comparisons across all schools, both public (government) schools, which comprise 71% of the total schools and are attended by 66% of the student population, and nongovernment schools (ACARA, 2010). Although the tests allowed parents to compare school results with the national data, parents did not necessarily know what to attribute to the school and what to attribute to the demographics of the students in that school. Responsibility for NAPLAN and for the development of public reporting of school-level results was given by the ministers of education in 2009 to a new statutory authority of the Australian Parliament, ACARA, which also oversaw development of the first national curriculum.

ACARA developed the *My School* website (www.myschool.edu.au) as the medium for school reporting. To prevent school ranking based solely on test scores, ACARA decided on value-added measures, which identify elementary, middle, and high schools that have consistently outperformed their peers with similar student populations over a 3-year period.

The *My School* site sought an approach that would be readily understood by teachers and parents. The site refrained from highlighting any one school as exceptional or providing metric estimates that are removed from the scales on which performances are measured (Organisation for Economic Co-operation and Development [OECD], 2008). An Index of Socio-Educational Advantage based on the education and occupation of parents of the students in a school was established. The site also took into account the proportion of students who were indigenous or from other backgrounds in which English was not the first language.

For each school, comparisons were provided with the 30 schools immediately above it and the 30 immediately below it on this scale. Comparisons were deliberately restricted to schools with students from similar socioeducational backgrounds. Within a school's comparison group, the schools whose students performed at the highest level demonstrated to the others that socioeducational advantage need not determine destiny. The high-performing schools in any category remove from the low performers the excuse that more cannot be expected of them given the kind of students with whom they work.

Informing School Improvement Strategies

Analyses, such as those above, show only that more might be possible for many schools, not what might be done to affect improvement. ACARA is currently identifying schools that have made substantial progress over the years in relation to their comparison schools. Independent evaluations are planned to identify specific practices that led to the schools' improvement.

Critics of NAPLAN and *My School* argue that the focus on literacy and numeracy will narrow the curriculum in schools, that teachers will waste precious time on test practice, and that the tests are too brief to provide precise enough measures with which to map individual students' growth over the years of schooling. The schools showing significant improvement do not, however, appear to have improved by narrowing their curriculum or through test practice but rather through a more coordinated role within the school in providing a consistently rich curriculum, with reading, writing, and mathematics used in many learning areas and with systematic use of school-based measures of student progress to personalize learning (Griffin, Murray, Care, Thomas, & Perri, 2010). Further, *My School* also reports on other aspects of a school, including school size, attendance rates, governance, the proportions of indigenous students and students with a language background other than English, information on the funding from all sources, public and private, and, in the case of secondary schools, some information on post-school destinations. It also includes a school's self-description and a link to the school's own website.

Accountability in itself does not yield school and system improvement. It shows what is possible, exposes weaknesses, and reveals where lessons could be learned that might facilitate school improvement, but more is needed.

Shaping Programs with a National Curriculum

Even though Australia is a high performer in international comparisons such as the Programme for International Student Assessment (PISA), a national curriculum is currently being developed for the first time in order to set higher national educational expectations. The curriculum is designed to cover K–12 for all learning areas, ultimately replacing the eight separate state and territory curricula. It sets out students' "learning entitlements" with content descriptions of knowledge, understanding, and skills. It leaves issues of pedagogy and the organization of learning to schools and, in cases where they exercise the authority, to school systems.

English, mathematics, science, and history for K–10 were all completed by 2011, with implementation now under way. The remaining K–10 learning areas will be completed by the end of 2013. Work on 11–12 is also under way. The curriculum is being published electronically (www.australiancurriculum. edu.au). For teachers, it is also being linked electronically to a substantial database of resources that can be searched through the structure of the curriculum (www.scootle.edu.au).

Public accessibility of the curriculum through its electronic publication gives parents explicit information on the full range of learning entitlements for their children. If a school is engaging in a misguided narrowing of the curriculum in the hope of influencing NAPLAN performance, that would be apparent to parents reviewing the curriculum.

International benchmarking during curriculum development has resulted in a curriculum that is more demanding than those it is replacing, particularly in mathematics and in primary school science and history. In elementary school English it brings a stronger focus on the nature of the language, including grammar, punctuation, and spelling.

Australian policymakers and the public are paying increasing attention to international, sample-based assessments of students' performance provided by OECD and the International Association for the Evaluation of Educational Achievement. They also focus on NAPLAN, because it is perceived to be crucial for learning.

References

Australian Curriculum, Assessment and Reporting Authority (ACARA). (2008). National Assessment Program. Available at www.nap.edu.au/

Australian Curriculum, Assessment and Reporting Authority (ACARA). (2010). *National report on schooling in Australia.* Sydney, Australia: Author.

Griffin, P., Murray, L., Care, E., Thomas, A., & Perri, P. (2010). Developmental assessment: Lifting literacy through professional learning teams. *Assessment in Education: Principles, Policy & Practice, 17*(4), 383–397.

Masters, G., Lokan, J., Doig, B., Khoo, S. K., Lindsey, J., Robinson, L., & Zammit, S. (1990). *Profiles of learning: The basic skills testing program in New South Wales: 1989.* Melbourne, Australia: Australian Council for Educational Research.

Organisation for Economic Co-operation and Development (OECD). (2008). *Measuring improvements in learning outcomes: Best practices to assess the value-added of schools.* Paris, France: Author.

CHAPTER 17

Rethinking a Century-Old System
Hong Kong

Patrick Griffin

The Hong Kong education structure emulated the British system for over a century. The system consisted of 13 years, culminating with the equivalent of the British A-level examination at year 13. Examinations, held at the end of years 11 and 13, were competitive and restricted the opportunities available to students who left at the end of year 11. The new Hong Kong academic structure and associated curriculum and assessment changes were initiated in response to four factors: (a) globalization and the impact of technology on work, society, and education; (b) pressure to develop 21st-century skills among the citizens; (c) Hong Kong's status as an international city with China's economic development; and (d) a need for citizens to be more aware of modern and historic China. In order to achieve the educational goals, there was a need to create multiple pathways to educational success and to remove the barriers that have traditionally restricted opportunities offered to students by the century-old system.

Contours of the New Academic Structure

The impetus and the blueprint for change came from the Hong Kong Education Commission, which in 2000 recommended an introduction of a New Academic Structure (NAS). It is comprised of a 3-year senior secondary curriculum and a 4-year undergraduate program with a goal to expand learning opportunities and to promote whole-person and lifelong learning. The Hong Kong government Education Bureau (EDB) recommended a new curriculum framework for basic education (elementary one to high school three), and the Diploma of Secondary Education (HKDSE) to replace the A-Level Examination and the Certificate of Education Examination. The change received widespread support as evidenced by an event where some 5,000 parents attended workshops in support of their children's reading and learning efforts at home. The shift in emphasis on a standards-referenced approach to assessment and curriculum was also recognized as a major innovation by Barber, Donnelly, and Rizvi (2012) in their report "Oceans of Innovation."

The new curriculum provides a "3 + 3" secondary education structure to ensure that all students have 6 years of secondary education. It replaces the previous two high-stakes examinations–the Hong Kong Certificate of Education Examination (HKCEE) and the Hong Kong Advanced Level Examination (HKALE). There is now one senior secondary examination, HKDSE.

The new curriculum has three components: the core subjects, the elective subjects, and the other learning experiences (OLE). The core subjects are Chinese language, English language, mathematics, and liberal studies. In addition, students take three elective subjects and OLE that aim to provide whole-person development. Specific learning goals cover the development of a broad knowledge base, generic skills such as language competency, critical and reflective thinking, and positive values and attitudes. OLE units focus on apprenticeships, community services, moral and civic education, and recreational activities. These skills are consistent with, and preempt, the widespread development of 21st-century skills (Griffin, McGaw, & Care, 2012).

The new academic structure provides an extra year of education to those who would have left after the HKCEE and makes it possible for all students to achieve higher levels of language and mathematical abilities, critical thinking, independent learning, and interpersonal skills. It also provides greater diversity and choice.

A second innovation is the Independent Enquiry Study (IES). It consists of three stages: project proposal (25%), data collection (25%), and the final product (50%). Despite the percentage framework, the IES is reported in a standards-referenced manner. It is regarded as important because it contributes 20% of the total marks for HKDSE, and it is oriented toward the kinds of skills that universities indicated they want from students. However, teachers' supervision experience and research expertise is limited. In order to move away from studies where data might be collected but the students have few or no skills in analyzing and interpreting them, teachers needed to be cautious about encouraging projects where their own lack of expertise is not exposed.

The first HKDSE examination in 2012 marked an important milestone in education reform, underpinning the local and international recognition of Hong Kong's revised education system. Approximately 71,000 students took the examination. The change was facilitated by the government's commitment to shift education in concert with the knowledge economy. Parental support was sought to sustain Hong Kong's performance on the Programme for International Student Assessment (PISA). Hong Kong also invested in its teaching force to help sustain the change in the curriculum.

Standards-Referenced Assessment and Reporting

A critical change in the Hong Kong education system was the introduction of standards-referenced reporting, which recognized what students could do rather than their relative standing among their peers. The standards-referenced reporting for Chinese and English language examinations was implemented in 2007.

There are five levels of performance, with Level 5 being the highest and Level 1 being the lowest. There is no official failure level. Level 5 is subdivided into three normative levels (5, 5*, and 5**). In a surprising shift in emphasis, a normative distribution is imposed at level 5. Less than 1% of students attain 5**. Of the candidates taking at least five subjects, 99.6% (68,703) obtained at least Level 1 or above, while 69.3% (47,831) obtained Level 2 or above in at least one of the five subjects, including Chinese and English language. Students taking five subjects with attainment at 3, 3, 2, and 2, in Chinese, English, mathematics, and liberal studies respectively were said to have satisfied the minimum entrance requirements for admission to government-funded higher education in Hong Kong.

This was a radical change in reporting for the Hong Kong education system. There are now no normative grades, no percentile ranks, no scores, and no pass or fail. Recognition of students' eligibility for employment or further education depends on the requirements set by different end users, such as prospective employers and tertiary education institutions. The introduction of school-based assessment in more subjects may also have caused increased supervisory and administrative workload for both teaching and nonteaching staff in the school—these issues yet to be fully addressed.

The new approach shifted the primary purpose of assessment from ranking and selection to recognition of skills. Most teachers and school department heads were familiar with the process of using work samples and descriptors in a standards-referenced framework, and their knowledge facilitated the change from a normative competitive grade and score-based system of reporting.

The new approach was also helped by teachers' confidence in their skill levels in discussing and comparing curriculum and assessment materials, moderating, and challenging one another about their conclusions. When the use of standards-referenced reporting was introduced in Chinese and English language studies in 2007, the initial focus was on the use of school-based assessment as a firm foundation for the new curriculum and assessment strategy. Many teachers had difficulty switching from norm-referencing, despite the fact that there was general agreement that the standards-referencing approach was an improvement. Many teachers, even senior and leading educators, continued to use the language of grades, so there was a need to remove the language of grading from the education rhetoric and to instead emphasize skills.

Changing Teacher Practices

Changing teacher practices in a culture embedded in tradition is difficult. Although teachers have embraced the framework of the new education system, many often divert to outcomes-focused rhetoric, consistent with content-based curriculum and grade-based assessment. As the new standards-referenced assessment system continues to unfold, it is important to show teachers how to use assessment data in a formative manner and to build their expertise in differentiated assessment and instructional strategies. Teachers need to understand that assessment is for their use in order to improve student learning, and that emphasis on traditional testing that supports a fixed body of knowledge needs to be interpreted differently or altogether abandoned.

Hong Kong is currently implementing school-based assessment that encourages teachers to observe student performance in a range of contexts over time. This change in assessment may lead to changes in teaching practices, but this will occur only if the teachers know how to use data to intervene in a standards-referenced framework. For that to occur, the implementation of the new assessment has to go beyond the current senior levels of schools, which perpetuate a two-tiered approach to assessment and reporting. Hong Kong has made great strides in its new assessments, its interpretation, and reporting. However, the standards-referenced assessment will encourage, but not ensure, changes in teaching and learning.

References

Barber, M., Donnelly, K., & Rizvi, S. (2012). *Oceans of innovation: The Atlantic, the Pacific, global leadership and the future of education.* London: Institute for Public Policy Research.

Education Commission, Hong Kong. (2000). *Learning for life, learning through life: Reform proposals for the education system—An education blueprint for the 21st century.* Hong Kong: Education Commission.

Griffin, P., McGaw, B., & Care, E. (Eds.). (2012). *Assessment and teaching of 21st century skills.* Dordrecht, The Netherlands: Springer.

CHAPTER 18

Quality Assurance System
Making Education Accountable in Russia

Elena Lenskaya

Over the last decade, Russia has undergone a significant transformation in its education accountability structure, from a decentralized, nebulous system toward a central assessment model designed to increase transparency and increase equity of post-secondary educational opportunity. The importance of this transformation was highlighted in many policy documents as well as in numerous public discussions (Dneprov, 1988; Pinsky et al., 2001). Russia has always taken pride in its educational system. Its mathematics and sciences curricula were among the most challenging, and the best Russian students often took prizes in international school Olympiads. However, little was known about the overall performance of Russian students and schools.

The Soviet System Legacy

The Soviet system of education was heavily standardized. The national curriculum specified the content for every subject area in a model disciplinary curriculum. Generally, there was just one school textbook for each subject area by grade level, prescribed by the Ministry of Education of each republic. Each textbook was accompanied by a very detailed teacher's manual containing lessons plans that were to be followed. The teaching process was standardized to such an extent that if two people simultaneously went to visit a classroom teaching the same subject at the same grade level in Moscow and Vladivostok, they were likely to see the same lesson. Of course, teachers did violate some of the prescriptions, but they never made those violations public.

Despite the prescribed curriculum, the outcomes were never specifically measured. The only assessments available were the "exam tickets": 30 to 40 questions in each subject that students had to answer to pass an exit exam. The exams were primarily oral with the exception of mathematics and Russian literature, where parts of the exam were in written form. No marking scheme was offered to schools; each school developed its own criteria. Given the lack of systematic assessment, higher education institutions did not trust the exam ticket grades and instead imposed their own systems of entrance exams. However, the university exam system was even less transparent: Each university administered its own entrance exam system, and neither the content nor the marking criteria were known to the potential students in advance. Universities often asked questions beyond the content of the national curriculum, and the applicants could not appeal a rejection, as their oral answers were not recorded.

The system of education was only accountable to the state. Education was free of charge, with the state being perceived as the only funder of education.

Introduction and Challenges of a New National Unified Exam

The Soviet assessment system was inherited by the newly independent Russia and survived for another decade. There were substantial complaints from students and their parents about the murky ways in which university entrance exams were administered. However, there was not enough political will to change the system. Given the university entrance exam system, the school exit exams had almost no purpose; the quality of outcomes across schools could not be compared, and the results were not relevant for the future careers of school graduates.

Thus, in 2001, the Ministry of Education made a decision to change the system and to introduce a new national exam called Unified Exam (UNEX) that would replace the former dual exam system (Ministry of Education for the Russian Federation, 2001). The exam was to be standardized and administered externally by a special quality assurance service. Students would take an exam in Russian language and mathematics and then select three additional disciplines in which to be tested. The new assessment had to serve two purposes: to give students an account of how well they performed while at school and to judge which of them should qualify for university entrance. This mix of purposes was seen from the very beginning by national and international experts as a potential threat to the validity of the exam.

The challenges the designers were confronted with were enormous. Their assignment was to design the marking scheme in such a way that students would take their exams in May, and all their results would be processed by the end of June, when students submit their college applications. However, the exam designers opted for a more comprehensive option, designing UNEX into three parts: multiple-choice items, open-ended questions, and an essay. The only exam that required oral examination was a foreign language assessment. The designers managed to meet the deadline requirements by a skillful combination of computer and manual marking and high-quality training of the markers.

Another challenge was to prevent cheating on the national exam day. Russia stretches across nine time zones. By the time children in the Far East finished their exam, children in the West still had hours to prepare. Therefore, each time zone had to have its own exam version.

The third challenge was accessibility of students from remote settlements. Transporting children to central exam stations was impossible, and the only solution was to send coded disks with passwords directly to schools and to test children there. This practice was found to be effective and provided equal opportunities for geographically challenged students.

UNEX was designed very rapidly; only 3 months separated the political decision from the first pilot tests taking place in four regions of Russia. The reason for such speed was due to the president of Russia taking a strong interest in the new scheme and wanting to take the university lobby by surprise. However, due to resistance by university leaders–who worried that the new system brought along with it a loss of control and a reduction in secondary income received from administering the entrance exams–the country-wide introduction of UNEX was delayed for 8 years.

The social impact of UNEX has been significant. The examination system is transparent, and all the exam data are recorded. Thus, corruption has become easily detectable, and authorities are taking action against cases of cheating. The transparency and accessibility of UNEX have had a positive effect on higher education trends. The ratio of students from Russian regions in most popular universities grew from 5% in 2000 to over 50% in 2012.

Unfortunately, the positive changes brought by UNEX have bumped up against the increasing use of the UNEX scores to rate school performance. UNEX scores have become one of the leading indicators used to judge the performance of regional governors, which leads to corruption, such as tampering with exam results.

After UNEX, standardized exams called the State Final Assessment (SFA) were introduced in 2009 in the 9th grade, at the end of the mandatory schooling stage. The procedure was similar to UNEX: All assignments were comparable in the level of difficulty and the results were equally protected from intrusion by the newly set up Federal Service for Supervision in Education and Research. However, because marking was organized by municipal authorities interested in demonstrating good results, the strictness of the marking procedure was at times violated.

The primary school exams will be introduced in 2015. These will be standardized in content, run by schools, and graded by municipalities. The content of these exams will be competence-based rather than knowledge-based. UNEX and SFA will be amended accordingly.

The next step in Russia will be to construct a reliable and effective national monitoring system. The plans are to monitor academic outcomes alongside social and communication skills necessary for personal success and social cohesion in a multicultural society. Russia will continue to participate in international assessments, thus providing important benchmarks of the overall national progress. These will be complemented by additional national and regional quality assurance evaluations.

The Impact of the National Unified Exam

The new standardized external exam has had a significant impact on the education system. Teachers have become more accountable for the results of their work and, even more important, they have started to think in terms of student learning outcomes. Previously, teachers focused on covering the required content, assuming that once they taught a lesson, students would learn it. Today, teachers are more aware of what their students know and do not know.

As time passes, UNEX is becoming more and more popular with parents. They are beginning to realize that the university entrance system is now more transparent and less corrupt. The government also appreciates the new, more reliable source of evidence that the system is functioning.

However, educators express concern that UNEX is perceived as an equivalent to a national quality assurance system and that other ways of measuring quality are not being properly explored. The country still does not have an appropriate national monitoring system or outcomes-based standards. As a consequence of such a lopsided policy, UNEX, while it contributes to equity and fairness, does little to improve quality of education.

References

Dneprov, E. (Ed.). (1988). *Koncepciya soderzaniya obshego srednego obrazovaniya* [*The concept of general secondary education*]. Moscow, Russia: VNIK Shkola.

Ministry of Education for the Russian Federation. (2001). *O sozdaniy soveta po organizaciyi podgotovki i provedeniya eksperimenta po edinomu gosudarstvenomu ekzamenu: Prikaz ministerstva obrazovaniya RF* [*On the set up of the UNEX preparation and pilot Council: The decree of the Ministry of Education*]. Moscow, Russia: Vestnik Obrazovaniya.

Pinsky, A., et al. (2001). *Strategia modernizaciyi soderzaniya obshego srednego obrazovaniya* [*The strategy for modernization of the general secondary education content*]. Moscow, Russia: Mir Knigi [World of Books].

CHAPTER 19

The Bottom-Up Push for Quality Education in India

Madhav Chavan and Rukmini Banerji

As in other parts of the world, there has been resistance to the assessment of learning outcomes in India. The old habit of creating provision-driven policy makes it comfortable for governments to hold themselves accountable for inputs rather than outcomes. Changing this habit is an uphill battle that has to be fought at every level, from villages to the national capital. This chapter offers an emerging model from India: an annual nationwide effort that aims to engage students, faculty, nongovernmental organizations (NGOs), women's groups, training and educational institutes, the government, and policymakers in understanding children's learning levels, using assessment for action as well as for accountability.

Development of the Annual Status of Education Report

In 2004, then newly elected government of India levied an education tax in order to substantially improve the funding of elementary education and declared that it would emphasize outcomes over outlays. However, there was no move on behalf of the government to publicly report on the effects of this additional education spending. Even the routine education data reported by the government were 4 to 5 years old in a country that was rapidly changing. Thus, Pratham, a large-scale nongovernmental educational organization, launched in 2005 a volunteer-based movement to conduct a national household survey.

The annual survey, called the Annual Status of Education Report (ASER), was designed to measure changes in student enrollment and learning levels. Each ASER is the result of collaboration among hundreds of NGOs, educational institutions, and volunteer groups—who reached out to nearly

320,000 households in 16,000 villages in order to assess and interview more than 700,000 children and parents. Every September and October, surveyors conduct fieldwork–the ASER is published and widely disseminated in early January of the following year. The cost of the entire exercise in 2011 was under $1 million; it was funded by individual and corporate donations (including Google and the William and Flora Hewlett Foundation). The ASER idea has been transplanted and adapted for use in nations in East Africa (Uganda, Kenya, and Tanzania), Pakistan, Mali, and Senegal.

The Impact of the Education Report

The first significant impact of ASER was the shortening of the lag time for data reporting: from nearly 5 years down to a single year. Until ASER came around, although it was common to talk about the poor quality of education in India, educational quality was never quantified. ASER brought to light two important facts in 2005 (Pratham, 2011). First, 92.4% of children in rural India were enrolled in school, and in almost half the country this number exceeded 95%. Second, nearly 48% of children in grade 5 could not read at a grade 2 level, and nearly 58% could not solve a simple division problem. Some states were worse than others, but a lack of basic skills was widespread.

The conclusion to be drawn from these data should have been simple for policymakers: A focus on basic reading and math outcomes was needed. But the reaction from the education establishment was to oppose the ASER assessment as minimalistic, to reject external assessments of any kind, and instead to propagate ideas of holistic learning that were not embedded in any measurable outcomes and were difficult to implement in the current Indian context.

Some states made attempts to improve the quality of education intermittently after 2005, but only a few focused on learning outcomes in reading and mathematics. At the national level, the government's focus on inputs continued with the passage of the Right to Education Act. As a result, subsequent ASER reports showed that, while the enrollment figures had improved to 97% by 2011, school attendance remained at around 70–75% (Pratham, 2011). And the estimates of basic learning in many states showed a declining trend.

Reality Check: India's PISA Performance

The lack of urgency or desire for change by the government was in stark contrast to the rapid changes in the country due to India's growing economy. Industries and businesses that were expanding complained that the youth who came to them for entry-level jobs, whether to serve at business counters, in hotels, or as engineers, did not possess basic skills. Change was needed. In

2009–2010, India entered the Organisation for Economic Co-operation and Development (OECD) Programme for International Student Assessment (PISA), which assesses children 15 years of age and older who are still in school. In India, this meant that about 60% of children were not a part of this survey, since they entered grade 1 but dropped out before age 15. Thus, it is no surprise that out of the 74 PISA participants, the two Indian states were ranked 72 and 73 respectively, higher only than Kyrgyzstan (OECD, 2009). The nodal scores of Indian participants for reading and mathematics literacy were the lowest on the PISA scale.

This is not surprising given the ASER data of the last 7 years. ASER was a simple assessment of whether a child could read a grade 1 or grade 2 level text, simple words or alphabets, or nothing at all. This simplicity allowed less-educated volunteers to assess with ease. Also, the results were so transparent that even illiterate parents could understand what they meant. Given this dismal student performance, how can an education system be built that focused on learning outcomes?

Learning to Read at Scale

It is often said that information leads to action. We do not find this to be true. Although information is a starting point for action, action itself must be engineered at all levels, especially when it concerns a disempowered population. A randomized evaluation conducted in Uttar Pradesh clearly highlighted the fact that merely informing parents and members of the community about children's learning levels, including testing children in front of them, led to no major changes in practice. However, when community volunteers are trained in "learning to read," children's learning levels improve (Banerjee, Banerji, Duflo, Glennerster, & Khemani, 2010). What is true of parents and village community members is true of policymakers, too. It is not enough to point out the problem. "What works" has to be demonstrated visibly at scale.

Pratham's Read India program, now instituted in nearly 25,000 villages, is attempting to improve the basic reading and arithmetic abilities of children in collaboration with village governments, village volunteers, and school teachers. This program was developed based on past experiences and evidence from randomized evaluations (Banerjee, Banerji, Duflo, & Walton, 2010). In each village, learning camps with a cycle of 7 to 10 days, 3 to 4 hours per day, are held every 2 to 3 months. The key elements of the Pratham "learning camps" include finding out the level of each child, grouping children on the same level together for instructional purposes, using appropriate teaching-learning methods and materials, and tracking the progress of each child.

There is a great deal of diversity across Indian classrooms in what children know and can do. The fact that a majority of children cannot cope with their grade-level curriculum means that teachers find it difficult to teach effectively. The key elements of Pratham's learning camps help remove some of these constraints. This short but outcome-focused, activity-based teaching-learning program takes children visibly from one level to the next. It modifies the role of information from merely starting a blame game to one that actually leads to immediate action and change. The idea is to generate a buzz that can help catalyze larger positive public opinion toward change and give high-level policymakers a chance to make a difference.

Focus on Learning Outcomes

As a result of clear goal-setting at the top and focused action on the ground, over the last decade there were impressive strides made in access and enrollment. This occurred because access to schools was equated with providing education. Measurable outcomes as indicators of good education had to enter this equation. Clear goal-setting and an alignment of policies with focused action inside classrooms was needed to go beyond universal schooling toward learning for all.

The isolation of schools from communities has to end. The language of "community participation" in education needs to be changed to "community initiative" for education. The stronger and more widespread this initiative, the more persuasive will be the pressure from below to build the capabilities of children and their ability to learn.

References

Banerjee, A. V., Banerji, R., Duflo, E., Glennerster, R., & Khemani, S. (2010). Pitfalls of participatory programs: Evidence from a randomized evaluation in education in India. *American Economic Journal, 2*(1), 1–30. Available at www.povertyactionlab.org/publication/pitfalls-participatory-programs-evidence-randomized-evaluation-education-india

Banerjee, A. V., Banerji, R., Duflo, E., & Walton, M. (2010). *Read India: Helping primary school students in India acquire basic reading and math skills.* Uttarakhand and Bihar, India: Pratham. Available at www.povertyactionlab.org/evaluation/read-india-helping-primary-school-students-india-acquire-basic-reading-and-math-skills

Organisation for Economic Co-operation and Development (OECD). (2009). *PISA 2009 results: What students know and can do.* Paris, France: Author. Available at www.oecd.org/pisa/pisaproducts/pisa2009/pisa2009keyfindings.htm

Pratham. (2005–2011). Annual status of education report (ASER). Available at www.asercentre.org

CHAPTER 20

Accountability as a Collective Professional Responsibility

Lorna Earl

Accountability has become the watchword of education; almost everyone agrees it is good, but there is little agreement about how it works or what it looks like. This chapter addresses professional accountability, focusing on classroom teachers and school leaders in their daily practice.

In 2000, Ken Leithwood and I described four models of educational accountability: (a) market competition, (b) decentralization, (c) professionalization, and (d) management approaches. The models were all focused on policy measures and were connected to monitoring, to large-scale assessment, to indicator systems, and used as measures of school improvement. However, large-scale assessments and accountability policies are proxy mechanisms designed to define and measure changes in student outcomes that are expected to occur as a result of changes in school practices. They are levers that policymakers have available to them, but they are gross measures far removed from the actions that really make a difference for students. Of all the school-based factors that can improve the learning of students in schools, teaching comes first, with leadership following close behind (Cuttance, 1998; Leithwood, Louis, Anderson, & Wahlstrom, 2004; Marzano, 2003; Robinson, 2007).

Accountability in education is more personal than assessment results and school report cards (Wagner, 1995); it is embedded in a relationship in which someone has a responsibility or obligation to account for, explain, or justify their actions to those who are entitled to it. The questions that emerge from this definition are: Who is accountable? To whom? For what? In what manner? Under what circumstances?

Professional Accountability: To Whom?

As Fullan (2003) reminds us, teaching is a moral enterprise, and the moral purpose of teaching is to enrich the lives of students. This moral purpose gives teachers and school leaders a very special accountability role. They are the individuals who work with students and guide their learning; structure and control assessment, evaluation, and promotion in school; determine eligibility for programs and activities; and foster students' sense of personal accomplishment and feelings of self-worth. Teachers are also the direct link with parents. From this perspective, I would argue that teachers and school leaders are, first and foremost, responsible to students and their parents.

Professional Accountability: For What?

Real accountability is much more than raising test scores. Linda Darling-Hammond (1997) said it simply, "Every child deserves a caring, competent and qualified teacher" (p. 5). Eraut (1994) identified professional accountability as a complex interplay of moral and contractual responsibility that includes quality, equity, respect, open relationships, and cost-effectiveness.

Quality in teaching depends on building and maintaining the specialized knowledge of the profession. Teachers should always be learning, growing, and changing their conceptions of the world around them, the role and nature of education, the material that they teach, and the implications for their daily activities. Each teacher is responsible for ensuring that his or her personal knowledge base is current, accurate, and comprehensive, and is reflected in the teaching and learning that occurs in classrooms.

Equity is deeply embedded in teaching and learning for each student in every class. Equity shows up in the kind of material that is available, the range of teaching approaches used, the pace of activity, assessment approaches, the feedback that students receive, and the alternatives that are available to foster deep learning for all students.

Accountability implies an ongoing, sustained, and open conversation between educators and the people who care about and pay for education, about what matters for students and their learning. These sustained and probing conversations between teachers, students, and parents provide an ongoing opportunity for mutual understanding and shared decisionmaking.

Cost-effectiveness in classrooms is mostly an issue of time. Time is a precious commodity for teachers and students. Time in schools is well used when students are engaged with their learning, using their knowledge and interests, and actively thinking about the issues at hand. Even modest increases in the amount of dedicated learning time can result in dramatic payoffs.

Professional Accountability: In What Manner?

If teachers and school leaders are responsible to the students they teach and their parents, then they must be adaptive experts, where professional learning is the routine core business of teachers and school leaders, in the service of the high-quality and high-equity schooling for students every day (Timperley, 2011). They must also engage in ongoing conversations that are rooted in trust and a willingness to be open to ideas and debate (Earl & Katz, 2006).

Professional Accountability: Under What Conditions?

Conditions to engage in the type of professional accountability described above are often rare; however, the most powerful support mechanism available to teachers and school leaders lies in their ability to think and work together to improve practices. Collaborative inquiry is one of the most powerful enablers of changes in practice to influence student learning (Katz, Earl, & Jaafar, 2009). As Fullan (2006) stated, the core of improving schools rests with professionals continuously improving learning and progress at all levels so that their collective efficacy enables them to "raise the bar and close the gap of student learning for all students" (p. 28). It is increasingly clear that deep and productive professional learning is critical to educational change. Deep professional learning requires active cognitive, emotional, and practical engagement from teachers (Timperley, 2011). As Timperley described it:

> Fundamental shifts in thinking about professional learning involve moving from professional development to professional learning, focusing on students, attending to requisite knowledge and skills, engaging in systematic inquiry into the effectiveness of practice, being explicit about underpinning theories of professionalism and engaging everyone in the system in learning. . . . Professional learning implies an internal process in which individuals create professional knowledge through interaction with this information in a way that challenges previous assumptions and creates new meanings. Challenge and meaning-making are essential because solving entrenched educational problems requires transformative rather than additive change to teaching practice. (pp. 3–4)

This kind of professional learning results from a process of focused collaborative inquiry:

> In collaborative inquiry, a group works together in repeated episodes of reflection and action to examine and learn about an issue that is of importance to them. Collaborative inquiry provides the process for problem framing,

evidence-collecting, reflection, revised action and reassessment. Engaging in collaborative inquiry allows educators to work together searching for and considering various sources of knowledge (both explicit and tacit) in order to investigate practices and ideas through a number of lenses, to put forward hypotheses, to challenge beliefs, and to pose more questions. It is the foundation of conceptual change as individuals come across new ideas or discover that ideas that they believe to be true don't hold up when under scrutiny. (Earl & Hannay, 2011, p. 190)

Personal Professional Accountability

Personal professional accountability is not easy in a context of government-mandated reforms that are intended to put pressure on schools through external quality control, with scores from large-scale assessment as the ultimate measure of success. Considering reforms dispassionately can be particularly hard when teachers feel denigrated, devalued, and under scrutiny. It seems that every intended outcome of a policy comes with its shadow of unintended outcomes, and the eclipse caused by the shadow is sometimes more dramatic than the original image. This being the case, teachers and administrators have it in their power to act, rather than react, and to move the educational change agenda forward in ways that they believe can benefit students.

If educators see student learning (not just test scores) as the most important outcome, and adopt a mindset of professional accountability that is grounded in providing high-quality teaching for all, they are compelled to engage in collaborative inquiry and professional learning and introduce high-leverage approaches to teaching and learning into the fabric of the reforms as they implement the reforms locally. Why? Because it matters!

References

Cuttance, P. (1998). Quality assurance reviews as a catalyst for school improvement in Australia. In A. Hargreaves, A. Lieberman, M. Fullan, & D. Hopkins (Eds.), *International handbook of educational change* (pp. 1135–1162). New York: Springer.

Darling-Hammond, L. (1997). Quality teaching: The critical key to learning. *Principal, 77*(1), 5–11.

Earl, L., & Hannay, L. (2011). Educators as knowledge leaders. In J. Robertson & H. Timperley (Eds.), *Leadership and learning* (pp. 186–201). London: Sage.

Earl, L., & Katz, S. (2006). *Leading in a data rich world.* Thousand Oaks, CA: Corwin Press.

Eraut, M. (1994). *Developing professional knowledge and competence.* London: The Falmer Press.

Fullan, M. (2003). *The moral imperative of school leadership.* Thousand Oaks, CA: Corwin Press.

Fullan, M. (2006). *Turnaround leadership*. San Francisco: Jossey-Bass.

Katz, S., Earl, L., & Jaafar, S. B. (2009). *Building and connecting learning communities: The power of networks for school improvement*. Thousand Oaks, CA: Corwin Press.

Leithwood, K., & Earl, L. (2000). Educational accountability effects: An international perspective. *Peabody Journal of Education, 75*(4), 1–18.

Leithwood, K., Louis, K., Anderson, S., & Wahlstrom, K. (2004). *How leadership influences student learning*. Minneapolis, MN: Center for Applied Research and Educational Improvement. Available at www.wallacefoundation.org/knowledge-center/school-leadership/key-research/Documents/How-Leadership-Influences-Student-Learning.pdf

Marzano, R. J. (2003). *What works in schools: Translating research into action*. Alexandria, VA: Association for Supervision and Curriculum Development.

Robinson, V. M. J. (2007). *School leadership and student outcomes: Identifying what works and why? No. 41*. Winmalee, New South Wales: Australian Council of Educational Leaders. Available at www.cred.unisa.edu.au/SILA/resource/frase9.pdf

Timperley, H. (2011). *Realizing the power of professional learning*. Berkshire, UK: Open University Press/McGraw Hill.

Wagner, R. (1995). *Accountability in education: A philosophical inquiry*. New York: Routledge.

PART V

WHOLE-SYSTEM CHANGE

Over the last several decades, countries across the globe have engaged in large-scale whole-system reforms. Although each nation has approached system-level educational change based upon unique educational, sociocultural, historical, political, and economic contexts, there are several strategies that have proved essential in creating meaningful progress, including a clear and inspiring national vision for education, strong leadership, consistent resource investment, professional capital development, internal accountability, focus on collective improvement, stakeholder engagement, and a positive outlook on change (Hargreaves & Shirley, 2009; Levin, Schwartz, & Gamoran, 2012). Whole-system change is gradual; however, as the chapters in this Part illustrate, such a process can have a profound impact on schools and students.

This last Part of the book tracks whole-system reform efforts among countries aspiring to continuously improve. The Part opens with Chapter 21, "Building the Collective Capacity for System Change: Professional Learning Communities in Wales," a provocative assessment by Alma Harris of the challenges and potential associated with building shared school-level capacity to create system-wide change. Harris tracks the development of Welsh professional learning communities and a national online portal designed to promote collective learning. She concludes with four lessons from Wales, arguing that what matters most is an investment in teacher quality.

Maria Helena Guimarães de Castro offers her perspective on the challenges associated with creating educational change in a developing international power. In Chapter 22, "Education in Brazil: New Challenges," she reviews the progress the Brazilian education system has made over the past decades of reforms but cautions that much of the improvement has focused on inputs rather than outputs due to resource constraints and cultural characteristics. She argues that several elements require attention—time spent in school, school structure, and teacher and principal quality–and, above all else, an educational vision that would mobilize the civic society, prioritize education, and invest in improving practice.

In Chapter 23, "Fifteen Years of Singapore's 'Thinking Schools Learning Nation' Vision," Pak Tee Ng posits that centralized strategic control and local tactical autonomy, paired with the country's commitment to educational investments and a high-quality teaching force, have led to a transformed education system, from a results-driven model to holistic learning education. Although he acknowledges the paradox of holistic education and the global push for standardized results, Ng concludes that what makes the country successful is its ability to manage the tensions associated with whole-system change and to continuously invest in education.

Analogous to Singapore is Chapter 24, "Fulfilling the Dream in Finland." Pasi Sahlberg traces the history of the Finnish system reforms and the impetus for educational change, and imparts lessons as to why Finland has been able to make substantial progress that today garners much global attention. Sahlberg argues that what made Finland a praised system was not an engagement in the Global Educational Reform Movement (GERM) focused on external accountability and standardization, but rather the country's focus on a dream of guaranteeing equal public education opportunities, investment in collective capacity-building, and utilization of positive drivers for change.

The book closes with the editor's conclusion, Chapter 25, "Conclusion: Issues, Challenges, and Lessons on Whole-System Reform." The chapter summarizes the main lessons from the book and acknowledges the importance of rethinking how we lead educational change.

References

Hargreaves, A., & Shirley, D. (2009). *The fourth way: The inspiring future for educational change.* Thousand Oaks, CA: Corwin.

Levin, B., Schwartz, R., & Gamoran, D. (2012). Learning from abroad: Rapid improvement is possible, even in a system like ours. In J. Mehta, R. B. Schwartz, & F. M. Hess (Eds.), *The futures of school reform* (pp. 13–34). Cambridge, MA: Harvard Education Press.

CHAPTER 21

Building the Collective Capacity for System Change

Professional Learning Communities in Wales

Alma Harris

As in many other countries around the globe, Wales is engaged in a series of reforms intended to significantly improve the performance of its education system. In 2007, the National School Effectiveness Framework (SEF) was introduced as the main driver for change and improvement. Within the SEF, the establishment of networks of "professional learning communities within, between, and across schools" was identified as a major lever for raising standards (Harris & Jones, 2010, p. 173). Since 2009, a national program of professional learning communities (PLCs) has been implemented in all schools. Although the PLCs are still operating, this chapter reflects upon the challenges, potential, and evidence to date about building this form of collective capacity to secure school and system-wide change.

Why System Improvement Leads to Little Change

In too many cases, strategies and interventions designed to improve schools and classrooms fail to make any real, sustainable difference to learners and learning outcomes. Although contexts inevitably vary, there are four core reasons why there has been so much innovation and so little improvement.

First, many of the approaches to educational reform still remain top-down. Often they are imposed on schools without sufficient or sustained attention to building the necessary capacity within the system to support and fully implement the change. Second, too much focus has been placed on external accountability, standardization, and punitive measures (Fullan, 2011), although research indicates that internal accountability, capacity-building, and support do more to improve performance than external factors (Hargreaves & Shirley, 2012; Mourshed, Chijioke, & Barber, 2010). Third, many of the well-meaning initiatives, innovations, and interventions generated by individuals operating at the policy level are disconnected from the classroom, where change matters most. Policymakers fail to take into account what is known about the most effective forms of instructional practice and discount the expertise of teachers who are best placed to advise and share what works. Lastly, so much of what passes for school and system improvement is still predicated on improving the system one school or one teacher at a time, which is slow, costly, and ultimately counterproductive. Large-scale improvement predicated on collective rather than individual performance has been shown to be far more effective. The high-performing systems already know this and invest heavily in generating social capital as a springboard to excellence (Hargreaves & Shirley, 2012). But what about those systems that are still aspiring to be better?

Wales: A System on the Move

Although much has been written about the highest-performing education systems such as Finland, Singapore, and Ontario, much less is known about the contemporary reform efforts under way in systems that are trying to improve. Russia, Malaysia, Australia, and Wales are engaged in concerted efforts to build the collective capacity for system-wide change and transformation.

In Wales, for example, a program of PLCs involving more than 1,800 schools and all 22 districts was introduced in 2009–2010. The national program defines a PLC "as a group of practitioners working together using a structured process of enquiry to focus on a specific area of teaching to improve learner outcomes and to raise school standards" (Welsh Government, 2011, p. 1). The national PLC model ensures that inquiry is disciplined and there is collective responsibility and autonomy. Schools have the latitude to select their own areas of inquiry, investigation, and innovation, but the nonnegotiable element is that their collective work has to benefit learners. Since 2009–2010, all schools in Wales were expected to form PLCs within their schools; however, without a clear methodology or model for teachers to use initially, the likelihood of a whole school becoming a PLC was reduced.

The Impact of Professional Learning Communities

Gauging the impact of PLCs is possible only if the PLCs use data to focus, guide, and inform their work. The most effective PLCs that operate within and between schools use student data to identify a specific need and then, subsequently, return to the same data to check on progress. This is one way to measure the PLC impact, but measuring impact at scale is more complicated.

To evaluate the overall impact of the national PLC work and to assist schools in making their collective PLC work more powerful, a national on-line platform was developed to enable all schools and professionals to connect, share, and co-create (Harris & Jones, 2010). Through this platform, PLC teams and members are able to upload and share important documents, access high-quality research and expertise, monitor their progress, engage in collective inquiry, and track impact as a natural part of their PLC work. The platform collects evidence at three levels: student, professional, and organizational learning. Because self-report is unreliable, claims about PLCs effectiveness have to be substantiated by relevant and reliable evidence and externally validated before the PLC work can be formally shared and published. If a PLC cannot demonstrate that it has made a positive difference to learner outcomes, the underlining goal, then it cannot be accessed by other professionals or schools.

The evidence about professional collaboration shows that despite much activity and hyperbole, very little of PLC work has made any real difference in learner outcomes. This is due to three reasons. First, a great deal of professional collaboration and networking is premised upon sharing existing practice rather than creating new or next practice. Networking is an effective means of story swapping and showcasing, but it is not the best tool to generate new ideas or knowledge. Second, most networking or professional collaboration has not been sufficiently rigorous; there has been no strong theory of action underpinning or guiding the work, so variability in practice and outcomes is the inevitable result. Third, many networks still rely on the frail links between individual teachers in schools to secure changes in practice. If sharing existing ideas is all that is desired, then networks are fine. But if the goal is to create rather than replicate, a more robust methodology is required. This is why the evidence-base on the impact of within-school PLCs is more reliable and extensive than that pertaining to networks (Vescio, Ross, & Adams, 2008).

The challenge of transforming an entire education system has to involve what actually works. If system reform is to be a reality, there is no room for fads. What matters is the degree to which teachers work together on teaching and learning. If the greatest resource any education system has is its teachers, then developing their skills, knowledge, and capability have to be the number-one priority. As Hargreaves and Fullan (2012) reinforce, professional capital is the new currency of improved school and system performance; it is best developed collectively.

Lessons from the Welsh System-Wide Reform

The approach to system-wide reform in Wales has been based on professional empowerment, respect, and a real sense that the profession is part of the solution rather than the source of the problem (Harris, 2011a). It is based on the growing research evidence around the world that teacher quality can be enhanced through improved collective, rather than individual, practice. But the continued discourse about underperformance on international benchmarking such as the Programme for International Student Assessment (PISA) and Progress in International Reading Literacy Study (PIRLS) is taking its toll. Some of the wrong drivers are now being grasped in an effort to force better performance out of the system. Some of the "third way" (Hargreaves & Shirley, 2012) thinking is still dominating the policy formation and implementation (Harris, 2011b). So what are some of the lessons?

First, there is a need to carefully calibrate the policy mix of pressure (accountability) and support (capacity building) within any attempt at system reform (Fullan, 2011). Both are needed, but it is important that they complement each other rather than compete for precious time, energy, and resources. Second, the unintended outcomes from policies need to be anticipated, as these can be more damaging and more powerful than the intended outcomes. Third, confusing the urgent with the important can lead to short-term solutions and ill-advised approaches that will fail to deliver. Focusing on the important—the children—is an antidote to pursuing foolish policies and replicating failed initiatives. Finally, the timescales and pressure for results that govern policymaking can encourage stop-start policies, create expedient rather than thoughtful decisions, and most important, fuel a disconnect between those formulating policy and those trying to make it work. In the fight between the ballot box and the classroom, the ballot box will always win. But putting teachers at the center, rather than at the periphery of the process of educational transformation, is one certain way of getting the right change and the right outcomes. Although there is no blueprint for system change, trusting teachers to lead reform rather than follow the contours of flawed policymaking is surely as close to ideal as we can get.

References

Fullan, M. (2011). Choosing the wrong drivers for whole system reform. [Centre for Strategic Education Seminar Series Paper, No. 24]. Available at www.cse.edu.au

Hargreaves, A., & Fullan, M. (2012). *Professional capital: Transforming teaching in every school.* New York: Teachers College Press.

Hargreaves, A., & Shirley, D. (2012). *The global fourth way: The quest for educational excellence.* Thousand Oaks, CA: Corwin Press.

Harris, A. (2011a). System improvement through collective capacity building. *Journal of Educational Administration, 49*(6), 624–636.

Harris, A. (2011b). System change: Realizing the fourth way. *Journal of Educational Change, 12,* 159–171.

Harris, A., & Jones, M. (2010). Professional learning communities and system improvement. *Improving Schools, 13*(2), 172–181.

Mourshed, M., Chijioke, C., & Barber, M. (2010, November). *How the world's most improved school systems keep getting better.* London: McKinsey & Company.

The National Assembly for Wales. (2001). The learning country: A paving document. Available at www.educationengland.org.uk/documents/pdfs/2001-learning-country-wales.pdf

The National Assembly for Wales. (2006). The learning country: Vision into action. Available at www.wales.gov.uk

Vescio, V., Ross, D., & Adams, A. (2008). A review of research on the impact of professional learning communities on teaching practice and student learning. *Teachers and Teacher Education, 24,* 80–91.

Welsh Government. (2011). Professional learning communities. Available at www.wales.gov.uk/topics/educationandskills/schoolshome/schoolfundingandplanning/plc/

CHAPTER 22

Education in Brazil

New Challenges

Maria Helena Guimarães de Castro

Brazil has made great advancements in basic education over the past 20 years and has set national goals for achieving international levels of quality by 2021. The 2009 results for the Organisation for Economic Co-operation and Development (OECD) Programme for International Student Assessment (PISA) showed progress among Brazilian students. Since the 2000 PISA, the country's overall score increased from 368 to 401, the third largest jump on record; however, the score is still far from the OECD/PISA average of 498. Among the 65 participating countries in the 2009 PISA, Brazil ranked 56th (OECD, 2009). This chapter examines the challenges associated with improving learning in Brazil.

The Current State of Education

Since 1995, the Brazilian federal government has focused on placing basic education (grades 1–12) at the heart of its strategic education agenda. Policies stemming from this agenda have led to successful efforts to advance universal enrollment in primary education, higher achievement levels (quality), reformulated financing mechanisms of education and increased investments, improved teacher career development and compensation, and a strong mobilization of civil society to place education as a national priority (Castro, 2011).

During this period, national assessments of school performance were also deployed. A series of tests, national exams, and indicators have allowed us to measure the evolution of student achievement and to set long-term goals. The new assessment data have helped diagnose problems and define their urgency and severity. In addition to the policies implemented by the

federal government, a series of initiatives was enacted by states and municipalities that effectively contributed to the reform, such as the expansion of
early childhood and secondary education.

Official 2011 data showed that 77.4% of all 4- and 5-year-olds are in
school, 98% of 6- to 14-year-olds, and 84% of 15- to 17-year-olds, although
only half of the older adolescents are enrolled at the high school level. The
average number of years of schooling jumped from 4 to 7.5, and the number
of students in higher education tripled (Castro, 2011). However, the results
from the latest national assessments indicate that the quality of the public
education system, which enrolls 86% of the eligible population, remains low.

According to the data released in 2012 by the Ministry of Education,
while mathematics and Portuguese levels at the elementary school level (1st
to 5th grade) show continuous improvement, average performance has stag-
nated in middle school and gotten worse at the high school level. Only 17%
of students finish middle school (9th grade) with adequate proficiency levels
in mathematics and 27% in Portuguese. By the end of high school, the situation is even more dramatic: Only 13% achieve adequate levels in math and
20% in Portuguese (Instituto Nacional de Estudos e Pesquisas Educacional
[INEP] [National Institute for Educational Studies and Research], 2012a).
In fact, of all students who enter high school, 40% drop out, and only 50%
complete their studies (INEP, 2012b). Data from the 2011 National Survey
by Household Sampling (PNAD) reveals that 16.3% of 15- to 17-year-olds are
not enrolled in school, a figure that has grown over the past 3 years (Instituto
Brasileiro de Geografia e Estatística [IBGE] [Brazilian Institute for Geography and Statistics], 2012). In sum, the data suggest that educational policies
implemented managed to expand access to school, but were not successful in
promoting student persistence, learning, or graduation.

New Challenges for Basic Education in Brazil

Conclusions drawn from international experience of educational reforms, and identification of some successful strategies, can guide the creation
of a new agenda for Brazilian education.

The first conclusion is that advancements in education are gradual, but
when interventions are well implemented and subject to course corrections
as the diagnosis improves and evidence is accumulated, good results are possible. Unfortunately, evidence-based research has not influenced the decisionmaking process of policy design in Brazil. It is known, for example, that
"time in school" is a positive factor in improving performance. However, due
to a combination of lack of political will, resource constraints, and, above
all, little pressure due to cultural characteristics (how "important" education
is seen by the general population), students stay in school, on average, 4

hours per day, with only 6.4% of students attending for full days. In general, parents are satisfied with Brazilian public education, and there is no pressure to increase quality among the great majority of the population. Parents are satisfied because there are school places for all children, free food for all, textbooks and didactic resources, uniforms, transportation, and so on. Probably such attitudes will change rapidly with the recent emergence of a new middle class, the decline of extreme poverty, and the demands of the labor market for more qualified workers.

Second, Brazil needs to diversify and change the architecture of its high schools. The Brazilian school model is unique: one mandatory encyclopedic curriculum for all. Classes are boring, far from the world of today's students. The system is also meritocratic; a school is considered to be good only if it manages to prepare a student for the most competitive "*Vestibulares*" (university entrance exams). Those who wish to obtain a technical degree are required to first complete high school or take classes outside of the regular school schedule, resulting in an extremely heavy workload. Thus there is an urgent need to simplify the curriculum, make it more relevant to today's labor needs, and offer diverse paths for both career and college opportunities.

Third, education is only as good as the quality of teachers and principals, and that is Brazil's primary challenge. The teaching profession is undervalued and wages are uncompetitive in the labor market. The current theory-based training is often removed from classroom instruction and daily practices, which leaves new cohorts of teachers unprepared for the job. The pay scale is also not merit-based, but rather governed by an equal pay policy. Thus, better-prepared school principals, with strong leadership skills, receive no extra compensation.

It appears clear that Brazil's quest to become a developed, sustainable country will only be viable if the country's educational system catches up fast. With 3.7 million children and youth out of school, combined with low school performance standards, Brazil will have tremendous difficulty remaining among the most prosperous economies, especially when the competition is investing seriously in education.

In order to address the three distinct challenges presented in this chapter—time in school, school model, and teacher/principal quality—as well as other key aspects that hold Brazil's educational system back, more and better-managed resources will have to be provided.

Luckily, a few states and municipalities, such as Minas Gerais, São Paulo, Ceará (states), and Rio de Janeiro (city), guided by effective and strong management at educational department levels, have recently demonstrated significant student achievement improvement by deploying innovative and consistent system designs aimed at specifically addressing the same core issues we face at the national level. Minas Gerais State, for instance, emphasizes teacher and principal certification, teacher performance evaluation, and literacy in primary schools. São Paulo State places a priority on curriculum and assessment with structured didactic materials to develop in-service teacher training. Ceará State focuses on school management, principal development, and literacy in primary schools. Further, the Rio de Janeiro Municipality uses a multipronged approach centered on curriculum and assessment, tutoring/mentoring for students, longer school days in favelas (shantytowns), and on a centralized system of tests administered every 2 months to all schools.

However, if these examples are to be scaled nationwide in an attempt to create substantive change, charismatic education-driven leadership must be present at the national level. For a country that neglected the education of its human capital for hundreds of years, a leap of quality will not happen with a gradual and noncritical mindset. Solutions to the problems are well known to the public, but the implementation of positive educational change at a national level will only happen when there is a collective will by Brazilian society at large to invest in education.

References

Castro, M. H. G. de. (2011). Q&A with Maria Helena Guimarães de Castro. In H. J. Malone (Ed.), *Lead the change series, No.7* (pp. 1–6). Washington, DC: Educational Change Special Interest Group, American Educational Research Association.

Instituto Brasileiro de Geografia e Estatística (IBGE) [Brazilian Institute for Geography and Statistics]. (2012). Pesquisa nacional de amostra de domicílios 2011 [National survey of sample households]. Available at www.ibge.gov.br/home/estatistica/populacao/trabalhoerendimento/pnad2011/default.shtm

Instituto Nacional de Estudos e Pesquisas Educacional (INEP) [National Institute for Educational Studies and Research]. (2012a). Resultados saeb/prova Brasil 2011 [Results of SAEB/PROVA Brazil 2011]. Available at www.portal.inep.gov.br/web/prova-brasil-e-saeb/edicao-2011

Instituto Nacional de Estudos e Pesquisas Educacional (INEP). (2012b). Censo escolar da educação básica 2011 [Census of basic education 2011]. Available at www.portal.inep.gov.br/basica-censo

Organisation for Economic Co-operation and Development (OECD). (2009). *PISA 2009 results: What students know and can do: Student performance in reading, mathematics and science, Vol. 1.* Paris: Author. Available at www.oecd.org/pisa/pisaproducts/pisa2009

CHAPTER 23

Fifteen Years of Singapore's "Thinking Schools Learning Nation" Vision

Pak Tee Ng

Singapore has earned a stellar reputation for its education system, having performed consistently well in the Trends in International Mathematics and Science Study (TIMSS) and the Programme for International Student Assessment (PISA). Two McKinsey reports classified Singapore as a system that is moving from great to excellent (Barber & Mourshed, 2007; Mourshed, Chijioke, & Barber, 2010).

Since the nation's independence in 1965, the Singapore education system has gone through several phases of development: a phase of standardization (mid-1960s to mid-1980s), a phase of local accountability (mid-1980s to mid-1990s), and a phase of diversity and innovation (mid-1990s to today) (Ng, 2010a). Reputed to be a robust system that promotes hard work and produces results, the present development phase of diversity and innovation appears to be a breath of fresh air in a standardized system. The inception of the phase can be traced to the launch of the overarching "Thinking Schools Learning Nation" (TSLN) vision in 1997, which is still operative today.

TSLN, introduced by Goh Chok Tong, who was then the prime minister, was a vision for developing a total learning environment by students, teachers, parents, workers, companies, community organizations, and the government (Goh, 1997). In this vision, schools are platforms for developing thinking skills and loyalty to country in students and society in general. The vision, which has become the basis of the national education policy, advocates for lifelong learning, creativity, and innovation. This chapter reviews the TSLN journey, 15 years after the vision first launched, by asking: How has education changed? What has not changed? What lies ahead?

How Has Education Changed?

The launch of TSLN was followed by various education reform initiatives designed to change the educational philosophy and the way the Ministry of Education (MOE) related to schools. A sample of the MOE initiatives are these: the 1997 National Education (NE); the 1997 Masterplan for Information Technology in education; the 1998 push away from an efficiency-driven education paradigm toward an ability-driven learning focus; the 2000 School Excellence Model (SEM), a self-appraisal model to replace school inspections; the 2004 "Innovation and Enterprise" (I&E) initiative, introduced to develop intellectual curiosity among students; and the 2005 "Teach Less, Learn More" (TLLM) program, designed to develop students into engaged learners and teachers into pedagogical innovators (Ng, 2008).

Underlying the various initiatives is a subtle shift in educational philosophy: from a focus on quantity to one on quality. Although TIMSS and PISA results show student proficiency in science and math, the results of these assessments underline the need to shift from a rote learning model to a differentiated instruction and engaged learning model that focuses on 21st-century skill acquisition (Ng, 2008; Tharman, 2005).

The meaning of quality became clearer through reviews of the primary, secondary, and post-secondary education. The 2009 Primary Education Review and Implementation (PERI) and the 2010 Secondary Education Review and Implementation (SERI) both recommended a rebalance of content knowledge acquisition and skills and values development. The aim was to move away from results-dominated education toward holistic education. There is now a dedicated Character and Citizenship Education (CCE) initiative, providing schools with guidelines and a CCE toolkit of current best practices. The Programme for Active Learning (PAL) provides primary school students with early exposure to different learning activities that would develop character and life skills, including sports, arts, and music. Secondary school students, during their crucial adolescent years, are given greater social-emotional support, career guidance, and opportunities to participate in athletics. The student-to-teacher ratio is set to improve, from 20:1 in 2009 to 15:1 in 2015 for primary schools and from 17:1 to 14:1 in secondary schools. Even in the area of Information and Communications Technology (ICT), the focus has now shifted to ICT integration in teaching and learning rather than merely infrastructural provision. The emphasis has shifted from tools to pedagogies, and from teacher usage to student empowerment (Ng, 2010b).

There is also a change in the way that the MOE relates to schools. Schools are now given more autonomy to decide their own strategies to fit their local context, with the MOE assuming a steering and supervisory role. The Cluster System, implemented in 1997, groups schools into clusters to foster greater collaboration and efficient use of resources for bottom-up initiatives. School inspections are replaced with self-appraisal through the SEM.

There is also a strong movement to increase the autonomy and professionalism of the teaching field. A number of "teachers for teachers" academies were set up to facilitate professional sharing and reflection among teachers (e.g., Academy of Singapore Teachers). This movement signifies a different relationship between schools and the MOE, and between practitioners and officials.

What Has Not Changed?

Paradoxically, for each change discussed above, there is something that has not changed (Ng, 2012a). First, although the educational philosophy has changed to emphasize quality rather than quantity, high-stakes examinations are still administered, partially as a result of global pressures to perform well on the international comparative tests, but also because of the culture: in which achievement in life is strongly linked with academic performance in school.

The society at large still perceives performance on high-stakes tests to be a determinant of a student's future (Ng, 2008). Under Singapore's meritocratic principles, high-stakes examinations at the end of primary and secondary education are inadvertently a key educational driving force. However, MOE is currently making efforts to promote holistic education, widen the definition of success, and provide more educational pathways. The problem is that the stakeholders may not be easily persuaded to change when the current strategy has delivered success (Ng, 2008).

Second, while schools are now more empowered, the government still holds the strategic power, and schools align themselves closely with official policies. Therefore, the empowerment strategy is more accurately described as "centralized decentralization" (Ng, 2010a, p. 284), where strategic control is held by the MOE to formulate national initiatives while tactical autonomy is given to schools for implementation. One reason is that the citizens hold the government accountable for the schools because they are government schools and "a failing on the part of schools is a failing on the part of the government" (Ng, 2010a, p. 283).

What Lies Ahead?

There are two factors that augur well for the future of the Singapore education system. First, education is still seen as an investment in the future and it enjoys generous governmental support (Ng, 2011, 2012b). To support PERI, MOE aims to provide all primary schools by 2016 with additional school facilities, including learning support spaces, indoor sports gymnasiums, dance and art studios, outdoor track and field facilities, and student health centers. The facilities will cost S$4.5 billion (US$3.6 billion) over 10 years. Despite the 2009 financial crisis, Singapore's national education budget increased to S$8.7 billion from S$8 billion the previous year (Ng, 2012b), thereby indicating that the government is committed to investing in high-quality education.

Second, the assumption that the education system is only as good as its educators has not changed. Over the years, the government has continued to strengthen the quality of its teachers and school leaders through stringent recruitment and various professional development platforms (Goh & Lee, 2008). All teachers, department chairs, and school principals are trained through the National Institute of Education, which works closely with MOE, ensuring consistency throughout the system.

If Singapore's education is considered successful, then its success comes as the result of the country's willingness to courageously face and navigate the many tensions and paradoxes of educational change, deriving creative energy from it (Ng, 2012a). Singapore succeeds also because it believes that education is an investment for the future and not just a current expenditure (Ng, 2011, 2012b).

References

Barber, M., & Mourshed, M. (2007). *How the world's best-performing schools come out on top.* London: McKinsey & Company.

Goh, C. B., & Lee, S. K. (2008). Making teacher education responsive and relevant. In S. K. Lee, C. B. Goh, B. Fredriksen, & J. P. Tan (Eds.), *Toward a better future: Education and training for economic development in Singapore since 1965* (pp. 96–113). Washington, DC: The International Bank for Reconstruction and Development/ The World Bank.

Goh, C. T. (1997, June 2). Shaping our future: Thinking schools, learning nation. Singapore Government Press Release. Speech given by Prime Minister Goh Chok Tong at the Opening of the 7th International Conference on Thinking, London, UK.

Mourshed, M., Chijioke, C., & Barber, M. (2010). *How the world's most improved school systems keep getting better.* London: McKinsey & Company.

Ng, P. T. (2008). Educational reform in Singapore: From quantity to quality. *Educational Research for Policy and Practice, 7*(1), 5–15.

Ng, P. T. (2010a). The evolution of school accountability in the Singapore education system. *Education Assessment Evaluation and Accountability, 22*(4), 275–292.

Ng, P. T. (2010b). Educational technology management approach: The case of Singapore's ICT masterplan three. *Human Systems Management, 29*(3), 177–187.

Ng, P. T. (2011). Singapore's response to the global war for talent: Politics and education. *International Journal of Educational Development, 31*(3), 262–268.

Ng, P. T. (2012a). An examination of school leadership in Singapore through the lens of the fourth way. *Educational Research in Policy and Practice, 11*, 21–34.

Ng, P. T. (2012b). The Singapore learning society: Intellectual capital development strategies and its response to the 2008/9 financial crisis. *International Journal of Learning and Intellectual Capital, 9*(1/2), 113–124.

Tharman, S. (2005, September 22). *Achieving quality: Bottom up initiative, top down support.* Speech given at the Ministry for Education, Work Plan Seminar, the Ngee Ann Polytechnic Convention Centre, Singapore.

CHAPTER 24

Fulfilling the Dream in Finland

Pasi Sahlberg

The Finnish educational transformation that began in the early 1970s was underpinned by an overarching belief that people should have equal opportunities and access to basic services, and that only through better-educated citizens can the nation catch up to its Western neighbors (Sahlberg, 2011). During that time, the country's Nordic neighbors were founding the Organisation for Economic Co-operation and Development (OECD), and Finland joined that family of prosperous industrial countries in 1969. The imperative for education reform changed due to a shift from an industrial- to a knowledge-based economy when Finland went through a rapid transformation of its economic structure during the 1980s and 1990s.

Unlike many other countries, being a world leader in education was never Finland's goal (Sahlberg, 2011). Aiming to be number one was not viewed as a realistic or an inspiring dream. Instead, the country's goal was to guarantee equal public educational opportunities to all Finnish young people all the way to higher education. Catering educational service to rapidly growing numbers of young Finns was a major economic burden for the government. Efficiency became a necessary principle in whole-system reform, especially during the 1990s financial crisis.

Successful implementation of the Finnish dream assumed that only highly educated teachers and leaders would be able to manage the challenges that the new, more diverse schools would bring (Sahlberg, 2011). Critical to the future success of the reform was to insist that all teachers have a research-based master's degree and that teacher preparation programs had to uphold substantial academic requirements integrating theory, content, and practice (Sahlberg). Students in these new programs were expected to master scientific knowledge and research methodology similar to any other study in Finnish research universities. Against all odds, teaching became an attractive career choice for a growing number of young Finns, who saw teachers as

Note: This chapter has been adapted from Sahlberg, P. (2011). *Finnish lessons: What can the world learn from educational change in Finland?* New York: Teachers College Press.

nation-builders for public good, not just instructors of individual interests. The growing interest in teaching also led to a newfound respect for the teaching profession in Finnish society, which helped support the educational reforms that the nation was undergoing.

The Finnish Way of Change

"The Finnish Way" of educational change is unique internationally. The Global Educational Reform Movement (GERM) in the United States, United Kingdom, New Zealand, and in many transition economies relies on externally mandated teaching standards with aligned standardized testing, stronger accountability for teachers and principals based on data from standardized tests, more school choice for parents, and integration of technology (Sahlberg, 2011). As a consequence, in these countries, schools find themselves in competition against one another. Finland does not subscribe to GERM.

The Finnish education system is attracting attention because it is fundamentally different from GERM; standardized tests are not the only criteria for assessing student learning, and reforms are not far removed from the classrooms. It is important to note that the best-performing education systems do not subscribe to the ideas of GERM, which dominate the education reform movement in the United States, United Kingdom, Australia, and New Zealand (Sahlberg, 2011). The top-performing systems—such as those in Finland, Alberta (Canada), South Korea, Japan, and Singapore—all assume that student learning can only improve through investment in educational equity, engagement of teachers, improvement of school leadership, and focus on developing social capital within the teaching profession (Sahlberg). Because Finnish teachers are prepared to improve their students' learning as well as their own work, the Finnish education system has improved steadily since the 1970s.

Lessons from Finland

The Finnish school system is one of the most studied in the world. Foreign researchers and journalists have played a key role in that. Analytical works by Sam Abrams, Linda Darling-Hammond, Andy Hargreaves, Tony Wagner, and several international journalists have helped propagate an understanding of the nature of whole-system reform in Finland, including components such as good teachers, inspiring curricula, and sustainable leadership. Let me offer three exemplary lessons.

The first lesson that Finland offers to other educational reformers is that whole-system reform can succeed if it is guided by an inspiring idea of the future that energizes people to work together for necessary change (Sahlberg, 2011). A frequently used example of an inspiring dream is that of Dr. Martin Luther King, Jr. His dream was not that the United States would have steady economic growth for some time to come. Dr. King's dream inspired people because it was emotional, ethical, and promised a better life for millions who had previously been disenfranchised from mainstream society. Similarly, being a top-ranked performer on international tests does not excite most educators. What the Finnish dream has focused on instead since the 1960s has been to provide every child in the country with quality public education regardless of family background, domicile, or personal ability. This goal inspired many stakeholders to come together and bring about educational and political changes. The Finnish dream looks like the vision that President John F. Kennedy had in 1961: to put a man on the moon and bring him back home safely by the end of the decade. His vision was also inspiring, challenging, and brave, and rewarded the entire nation through its outcomes (Sahlberg).

The second lesson from Finland concerns teachers. Finnish teachers are the foundation for the country's overall high education performance. What is significant in the Finnish approach to teacher policies is that it has focused on improving the professional knowledge and skills of teachers and leaders as a collective group, not only as individual practitioners. Teachers collaborate with one another. Finnish education policies have systematically focused on improving schools as human organizations with a moral mission, rather than seeing schools as academic training camps with mostly instrumental value for individuals. Educational reform in Finland builds social capital within the system in concert with individual professional development and growth (Sahlberg, 2011).

The third lesson to take away from Finland is the importance of focusing on positive drivers of educational change, as opposed to the wrong drivers of change as embodied in the world today by the GERM (Fullan, 2011). Countries infected by the GERM build their education reforms on interrelated changes, standardization of teaching and learning, test-based accountability, merit-based teacher pay, and privatization of public schools for more school choice as keys to turning around unsatisfactory school systems (Sahlberg, 2011). The GERM embeds the ethos of competition in education on the expense of cooperation and community.

Finland remains immune to this worldwide virus mostly because of its academically homogeneous teaching cadre. All high-performing educational systems have designed their reform architecture on systemic strategies that rely on better equity in education, collective professional and institutional improvement, and enhanced teaching and learning in schools (Sahlberg, 2011). Many education reform experts believe that nationwide goals to improve quality and equity in education in any system will not be met with the policies similar to those of GERM. "The Finnish Way" suggests that these policies are simply wrong starting points for whole-system reforms.

Educational Change Today

Global benchmarking of education systems has radically changed the geography of education in the world (Sahlberg, 2011). Before 2000, the United States and other Anglo-Saxon countries led in research, innovation, and high educational performance. Now several Asian countries, Canada, and Finland are in the limelight as educational models for continued improvement (Hargreaves & Shirley, 2012). It is not surprising that most OECD countries wish to be among the top education nations in the future. This standardized global race for excellence judged by standardized international tests has visible rewards and consequences to both policy and practice in many countries (Sahlberg).

The negative aspect of the growing emphasis on international rankings is that it leads to governing education by numbers rather than values. It favors education policies that focus on *narrowing the achievement gaps* and *raising the bar* (Sahlberg, 2011). Such policies focus on setting clear targets for student performance, designing external standardized tests to measure students' and teachers' performance, rewarding and sanctioning achievement scores, and publicly ranking schools for the sake of accountability. This has without question increased competition, standardized solutions, and market-based models to achieve set policy goals (Sahlberg). At the same time, educational research and media report about the unintended consequences of pressure on teachers and children: narrowing curricula, increased teaching to tests, teachers leaving their jobs, corruption, and student suicides due to harder performance expectations. The GERM is causing serious damage in already struggling education systems.

Overemphasis of international rankings leads to an assumption that talent development in today's complex societies is about improving people's academic performance and basic skills. It is paradoxical that on the one hand education reformers offer more parental choice and on the other hand judge student achievement by using standardized performance criteria, without any choice for students to show how they feel about what they do or what other competences they may have. This leaves little room for innovation in schools. Standardization and teaching-to-the-test will not increase the flexibility, risk-taking, or creativity in schools that are the key conditions for making schools places where each young individual could explore and discover his or her own talents (Sahlberg, 2011).

The Finnish education system offers an alternative approach to the GERM view of education. First, we, the world, do not need to privatize public schools to develop innovative educational changes in our school systems (Sahlberg, 2011). Trust in schools and teachers, enhanced leadership, and more flexibility could lead to inspired and productive learning for all. Second, we should utilize pedagogical innovations that have been developed since the 1960s. We know enough about powerful teaching, effective schools, and insightful leadership to make our public school systems work better (Sahlberg). Finland has been an interesting laboratory for implementing educational innovations (many of the innovations developed in the United States) for a large-scale education reform.

References

Fullan, M. (2011). Choosing the wrong drivers for whole system reform. [Centre for Strategic Education Seminar Series Paper, No. 24]. Available at www.cse.edu.au

Hargreaves, A., & Shirley, D. (2012). *The global fourth way: The quest for educational excellence.* Thousand Oaks, CA: Corwin Press.

Sahlberg, P. (2011). *Finnish lessons: What can the world learn from educational change in Finland?* New York: Teachers College Press.

CHAPTER 25

Conclusion:
Issues, Challenges, and Lessons
on Whole-System Reform

Helen Janc Malone

Change is a dynamic and, at times, difficult process. Our tendency is to gravitate toward existing practices, familiar institutional systems, and known expectations. We perceive externally driven change as a directive, an imposition, an intrusion, and a disruption to our daily work. We tend to embrace change when we can co-construct it, when it is meaningful and purposeful to us, when it is in line with our values and beliefs, and when we see its potential to genuinely improve our existing condition(s). Thus, positive change tends to flourish in environments that are inspiring and inclusive, that negotiate internal and external expectations, and that empower all stakeholders along a path toward shared goals and outcomes (Fullan, 2011; Hargreaves & Shirley, 2012).

The purpose of this book is to offer reflections on the issues, challenges, and lessons of change within the education sector, as led, examined, and practiced by top leaders in global education thought. This book addresses some of the core components necessary to lead educational change and openly discusses the ramifications and triumphs that come along with such an endeavor.

Issues and Challenges

Over the past couple of decades education has been undergoing a global paradigm shift. Informed by a growing international interdependence, labor market shifts, changing political dynamics, and increasingly complex social arrangements, the education sector has focused on ways it can respond to external expectations. Although the environmental factors might appear similar on the surface, the cultural, historical, economic, institutional, and political realities have moved each nation along a unique path of educational change. Some systems have focused on equity, access, and educational justice as a way to mitigate years of segregation and oppression; some have centered on standardization and external accountability as the driving forces that could help a nation stay competitive in the international marketplace; and still others have moved away from centralization and a concentration on the basics (reading and math), paying attention instead to holistic education as a desired approach to help prepare students for the emerging knowledge-based global economy.

Educational change is inevitably a political process that has a tendency to be episodic, driven by external policies, susceptible to electoral cycles, and reactive to outside pressures. When there is synergy between the education sector and external environments, positive outcomes can be realized. However, there can also be a misalignment of what Fullan (2011) refers to as pressure and support. As Payne (2008) argues, educational change becomes contentious when there is a culture of low expectations, distrust in and among educators, a lack of institutional learning, and a continued focus on preserving existing institutional arrangements and power structures.

Amid these constraints and challenges, how can we lead system-wide educational change in a meaningful way? The authors in this anthology believe that change for the better is possible when we engage diverse stakeholders, empower practitioners, build professional capacity, align internal and external accountability structures, and challenge the existing narratives and structures that prevent equitable access to learning opportunities.

Lessons

The book is organized into five Parts, each Part imparting important lessons about how to lead educational change. Below I offer a summary of the major points. They are not all-encompassing, but rather are designed to start a conversation about leading meaningful educational change.

The growing global focus on international benchmarking and standardized tests have created a culture of competition and comparisons between nations. As Schleicher (Chapter 1) observes, PISA has become a leading measure applied to inform educational policies, sparking important conversations about equity and quality, societal goals and expectations. Hargreaves (Chapter 2), however, argues that international benchmarking has also led to the pursuit of higher test scores, which is not a stimulating, long-term goal. He advocates instead for a *fourth way* approach to educational change, one comprised of such principles as: pursuing an inspiring dream, entrusting schools to serve as a public good, encouraging change and innovation from within schools, and focusing on learning beyond tests.

Zhao (Chapter 3) also cautions us about standardization and centralization as the main tenants of education policy. He reminds us that what produces engaged citizens is focus on innovation, creativity, and entrepreneurship. Shirley (Chapter 4) offers another emerging consideration in education policy, that of harmonization with technology, whereby technology is utilized to supplement, not supplant, quality teaching. I close Part I (Chapter 5) by encouraging us to think about change beyond the immediate market demands, to embrace a broader definition of learning, and to actively involve front-line stakeholders—teachers, students, families, and communities—in the process of education reform and improvement.

The second Part of the book is dedicated to improving practice. Stoll (Chapter 6) encourages us to nurture school cultures that honor innovation and continuous professional capacity building. Spillane (Chapter 7) advocates for a distributed leadership perspective—a framework focused on diagnostic and design work that propels school staff toward shared aspirations and goals. Anderson (Chapter 8) too, reminds us that deep learning is best promoted through professional learning communities, and as Lieberman (Chapter 9) offers, through professional development experiences that create platforms for dialogue, reflection, and joint learning. Cámara (Chapter 10) closes Part II with a vignette illustrating how personalizing educational experiences through tutorial relationships empower students and improve practice by rethinking the relationship between educators and learners. Collectively, the authors of Part II argue for a cultural shift within our schools, one that moves us toward collaborative work environments, mutual trust, engagement in the communities of practice, and a continuous knowledge-building/-sharing/-transfer.

Part III of the book conveys that leading educational change is also about directly addressing issues of equity and educational justice, working to transform the systemic and structural power arrangements that have historically perpetuated learning barriers in underserved communities. As Jansen asks, "how does a public school make available the highest education standards to all learners while at the same time ensuring optimal access and success to the whole student body?" Ainscow begins to unpack this question in Chapter 11, arguing that ecology of equity plays a critical role in establishing environments that support student development and learning. He argues that educational change must address within-, across-, and beyond-school factors. Datnow (Chapter 12) thus urges policymakers, educators, and researchers to work collectively and to address the intersection of education and equity in order to support underserved students. As the last three chapters of this

Part express–Deckman (Chapter 13), Jansen (Chapter 14), Gvirtz and Torre (Chapter 15)–establishing an equity–excellence balance in countries that have historically undermined educational justice requires that societies, and more specifically educators, directly address the power structures that propagate systemic inequity and ensure that a broader set of actors are involved in policy construction and are invested in new institutional practices that create accessible, equitable, high-quality education for all students.

As discussed in Part IV, educational accountability structures emerging around the globe are serving to increase transparency, identify schooling systems' weaknesses and strengths, and inform the public and decisionmakers about students' knowledge base (McGaw, Chapter 16). As Griffin (Chapter 17) and Lenskaya (Chapter 18) explain, meaningful assessments are being designed to address students' outcomes in cross-disciplinary learning and skills acquisition and do not serve a mere punitive function. Measurable outcomes help to clarify goals, align policies and systems, and focus action in schools (Chavan and Banerji, Chapter 19). However, as Earl (Chapter 20) concludes, external accountability is "a proxy mechanism" for policymakers. What is also needed, she argues, is professional accountability that supports student learning through quality instruction. Together, synergy between internal and external accountability is necessary in order to inform and improve practice.

So, how do we create spaces for professional capacity building, investments in equity and educational justice, and engagement in both internal and external accountability? That is the question tackled by the authors in Part V. As Harris (Chapter 21) notes, accountability and capacity-building strategies should complement each other, and focus on improving instruction and learning in the long-term over short-term policy-driven goals. As Harris, Castro, Ng, and Sahlberg note in their chapters: (a) civil society should rally around a shared vision of what it wants for its future and for its students; (b) teaching and learning should be front and center in the educational change process; (c) building internal capacity and empowering teachers and administrators should be salient to the creation of collaborative and innovative schooling environments; (d) investing in educational change should not be subject to election cycles; rather, it should be an ongoing social investment designed to support all learners; and (e) the focus of change should be on positive, rather than punitive, drivers of change (Fullan, 2011; Hargreaves & Shirley, 2012, Harris, 2011).

Leading Change

As you think about leading educational change in your community, consider the following questions: What goals are you trying to achieve? What impact do you want to have on your students? What resources do you currently have at your disposal to leverage meaningful change? What policy, political, and institutional constraints or opportunities exist that can hinder or nurture your efforts? How do you encourage innovation and practice-driven design work? How you define and approach the change process will speak to the value you place on education, the trust you have in educators in your community, and the vision you hold for what student learning could and should be. It will also speak to the guiding principles, assumptions, and philosophies that inform your educational change process. I hope this book encourages you to lead meaningful educational change in your community.

References

Fullan, M. (2011). Choosing the wrong drivers for whole system reform. [Centre for Strategic Education Seminar Series Paper, No. 24]. Available at www.cse.edu.au

Hargreaves, A., & Shirley, D. (2012). *The global fourth way: The quest for educational excellence.* Thousand Oaks, CA: Corwin Press.

Harris, A. (2011). System change: Realizing the fourth way. *Journal of Educational Change, 12,* 159–171.

Payne, C. M. (2008). *So much reform, so little change: The persistence of failure in urban schools.* Cambridge, MA: Harvard Education Press.

About the Editor
and Contributors

Helen Janc Malone (Editor) has conducted research on out-of-school time and expanded learning, college readiness, and system-level educational change at Harvard University. She is a cofounder of two American Educational Research Association's (AERA) special interest groups, on out-of-school learning and on school reform. Her recent publications include "Addressing the Disadvantages of Poverty: Why Ignore the Most Important Challenge of the Post-Standards Era?" (with Henig & Reville, a chapter in *The Futures of School Reform*, Harvard Education Press, 2012), *Expanded Learning Time and Opportunities* (Jossey-Bass, 2011), and *Lead the Change Series* (AERA Educational Change Special Interest Group, 2011–2012).

Mel Ainscow is professor of education and co-director of the Centre for Equity in Education at the University of Manchester, United Kingdom. His work focuses on inclusion, teacher development, and school improvement. His recent books, all from Routledge, include *Developing Equitable Education Systems* (with Dyson, Goldrick, & West, 2012), *Responding to Diversity in Schools: An Inquiry Based Approach* (with Miles, 2010), and *Improving Schools, Developing Inclusion* (with Booth, Dyson, & Farrell, 2006). He was made a commander of the British Empire in recognition of services to education in the queen's 2012 New Year honors list.

Stephen E. Anderson is professor of Educational Administration at the Ontario Institute for Studies in Education University of Toronto. His research focuses on school improvement at the classroom, school, and district levels internationally (North and South America, Africa, and South Asia). His recent chapters include "Linking Leadership to Student Learning" (Leithwood & Louis, Jossey-Bass, 2011), "Moving Change: Evolutionary Perspectives on School Improvement" (Fullan, Springer, 2005), and "Primary and Secondary Education: Studies of School Improvement in Developing Countries" (Peterson, Baker & McGraw, Elsevier, 2010).

Rukmini Banerji is director of the Assessment Survey Evaluation Research (ASER) Centre in New Delhi, India, and is also a senior member of Pratham's national leadership team. She is a former Rhodes Scholar, has worked in the past as a program officer for the Spencer Foundation in Chicago, and has done postdoctoral research at the Population Research Center at the University of Chicago. Her work has focused on designing, implementing, and analyzing large-scale initiatives that aim to improve student learning in primary schools in India.

Gabriel Cámara is the founder of Convivencia Educativa, A.C. (now Redes de Tutoría, S.C.), a group of researchers-promoters that conducts educational projects with public and private agencies. His recent books include *Otra Educación Básica es Posible* [*Another Basic Education Is Possible*] (2008), *Enseñar y Aprender con Interés* [*Teaching and Learning with Interest*] (2006), *Comunidad de Aprendizaje: Cómo Hacer de la Educación Básica un Bien Valioso y Compartido* [*Learning Community: How to Make Basic Education and Sharing a Valuable Asset*] (2004), all published by Siglo XXI Editores.

Maria Helena Guimarães de Castro is a retired professor of political science at the State University of Campinas/Brazil, an associate researcher of the Center for Public Policies, and executive director of SEADE, a public foundation of the State of São Paulo responsible for the production and analysis of social and economic data. She is a member of the Academic Council of the National Association of Educational Evaluation and the Brazilian Academy of Education.

Madhav Chavan is the cofounder and CEO of Pratham, the largest nonprofit in India dedicated to providing high-quality education to underprivileged children. Prior to this post, he served on India's Prime Minister's National Advisory Council in India. Originally a reader at the University Department of Chemical Technology in Mumbai University, he also studied at the University of Houston, and has been a visiting fellow at both the Chinese Academy of Sciences and at Queensland University of Technology. His work focuses on issues of children's educational and youth skill development in India.

Amanda Datnow is professor and chair of the Department of Education Studies at the University of California, San Diego. Her research focuses on the politics and policies of school reform, particularly with regard to the professional lives of educators and issues of equity. She is on the editorial board of several journals, and was the editor-in-chief of the *Journal of Educational Change*. She also consults for professional organizations and government agencies.

Sherry L. Deckman is assistant professor of education at Ithaca College in New York, where she teaches social and cultural foundations of education. Her research explores diversity in higher education and professional development for educators related to addressing inequity. Her recent publications include "But What Can I Do? Three Necessary Tensions in Teaching Teachers About Race" (with Pollock, Mira, & Shalaby, *Journal of Teacher Education*, 2010) and *Humanizing Education: Critical Alternatives to Reform* (with Cooper, Dobbs, Francois, Nikundiwe, & Shalaby, Harvard Educational Press, 2010).

Lorna Earl is president of Lorna Earl and Associates and a part-time professor at the University of Auckland. She has retired as a professor in the Theory and Policy Studies Department and as a head of the International Centre for Educational Change at the Ontario Institute for Studies in Education, University of Toronto. As a leader in the field of assessment and evaluation, she has written books, chapters, and articles about assessment, using data for decisionmaking, evaluation methods, knowledge mobilization, and networking for school improvement.

Patrick Griffin is chair of Education at the University of Melbourne, director of the Assessment Research Centre, and the associate dean of the Melbourne Graduate School of Education. He is a project team leader for UNESCO in southern Africa, a World Bank consultant in Vietnam and China, and the executive director of the Assessment and Teaching of 21st Century Skills Project. His most recent book is *Assessment and Teaching of 21st Century Skills* (with McGaw & Care, Springer, 2012).

Silvina Gvirtz is general executive director of Conectar Igualdad, professor at Universidad de San Martín, visiting professor at SUNY–Albany, and researcher at the National Scientific and Technical Research Council (CONICET). Previously, she served at the Ministry of Education of Buenos Aires province. Her recent books are *Political Participation and School Government: The Cases of Brazil and Nicaragua* (Cortes Editora, Brazil, 2012) and *How to Build a Good School: Tools for the School Principal* (Editorial Aique, Argentina, 2011).

Andy Hargreaves is the Thomas More Brennan chair in the Lynch School of Education at Boston College. His books have earned outstanding writing awards from the American Educational Research Association, the American Library Association, the National Staff Development Council, and the American Association of Colleges for Teacher Education. His most recent books are *Professional Capital: Transforming Teaching in Every School* (with Fullan, Teachers College Press, 2012) and *The Global Fourth Way: The Quest for Educational Excellence* (with Shirley, Corwin, 2012).

Alma Harris is professor and director of the Institute of Educational Leadership at the University of Malaysia and the president of the International Congress of School Effectiveness and School Improvement. From 2008, she was the pro-director (Leadership) at the Institute of Education, London, and in 2010–12 she was a senior policy advisor to the Welsh government. Her research work focuses primarily on leading organizational change and development. Her book, *Distributed Leadership in Schools: Developing the Leaders of Tomorrow* (Routledge & Falmer Press, 2008), has been translated into several languages.

Jonathan D. Jansen is vice chancellor and rector of the University of the Free State in central South Africa, president of the South African Institute of Race Relations, and a distinguished scientist fellow at the Academy of Science for the Developing World. His research focuses on reconciliation efforts and on assisting disadvantaged schools in changing their culture and performance. His recent books include *Great South African Teachers* (Bookstorm, 2011), *We Need to Talk* (Pan Macmillan, 2011), and *Knowledge in the Blood* (Stanford University Press, 2009).

Elena Lenskaya is dean of education at the Moscow School of Social and Economic Sciences and a World Bank consultant on education programs involving assessment and quality assurance. She was previously the chair of the Open Society Institute General Education sub-board, assistant director for Education and English Language teaching at the British Council, and an advisor to the Minister of Education of Russia. In 2007, she was awarded the Order of the British Empire.

Ann Lieberman is a senior scholar at SCOPE (Stanford Center for Opportunity Policy in Education) and SCALE (Stanford Center for Assessment, Learning & Equity), and professor emeritus at Teachers College, Columbia University. She is widely known for her research on teacher leadership and development, collaborative research, and school-university partnerships. Among her recent books are *Mentoring Teachers: Navigating the Real World Tensions* (with Hanson & Gless, Jossey-Bass, 2012) and *How Teachers Become Leaders: Learning from Practice and Research* (with Friedrich, Teachers College Press, 2010).

Barry McGaw is a vice chancellor's fellow at the University of Melbourne and chair of the Australian Curriculum, Assessment and Reporting Authority. He was the founding executive director of the international Cisco-Intel-Microsoft Assessment and Teaching of 21st Century Skills project, director for Education at the Organisation for Economic Co-operation and Development (OECD), and executive director of the Australian Council for Educational Research (ACER). His research interests include educational measurement, curriculum and assessment in upper secondary education, and policies to enhance equity in education.

Pak Tee Ng is associate dean of Leadership Learning and the head of Policy and Leadership Studies Academic Group at the National Institute of Education (NIE), Nanyang Technological University (NTU), Singapore. He has written extensively about school leadership and education policy and reform in Singapore. He is currently the executive editor of *Educational Research for Policy and Practice*, the flagship journal of the Asia-Pacific Educational Research Association. He is also an editorial board member of several other international refereed journals.

Pasi Sahlberg is director general of CIMO (Centre for International Mobility and Cooperation) in Helsinki, Finland. He is a board member of IASCE (International Association for Study of Cooperation in Education) and ASCD (Association for Supervision and Curriculum Development), and is an adjunct professor of education at the University of Helsinki and the University of Oulu in Finland. His award-winning book is titled *Finnish Lessons: What Can the World Learn from Educational Change in Finland* (Teachers College Press, 2011).

Andreas Schleicher is deputy director for Education and Skills and a special advisor on Education Policy to the secretary-general at the Organisation for Economic Co-operation and Development (OECD). As head of OECD's programs on indicators and analysis, he oversees the Programme for International Student Assessment (PISA), the OECD Survey of Adult Skills (PIAAC), the OECD Teaching and Learning International Survey (TALIS), and the development and analysis of benchmarks on the performance of education systems (INES).

Dennis Shirley is professor of education and senior associate at the Center for the Study of Testing, Evaluation, and Education Policy at the Lynch School of Education, Boston College. He is the editor-in-chief of the *Journal of Educational Change* and chair of the special interest group on Educational Change of the American Education Research Association. His recent books include *The Global Fourth Way* (with Hargreaves, Corwin, 2012), *The Fourth Way* (with Hargreaves, Corwin, 2009), and *The Mindful Teacher* (with MacDonald, Teachers College Press, 2009).

James P. Spillane is the Spencer T. and Ann W. Olin Professor in Learning and Organizational Change and professor of Human Development and Social Policy at the School of Education and Social Policy, Northwestern University. He is also a faculty fellow at the Institute for Policy Research and Principal Investigator at the Distributed Leadership Studies. His recent work includes *Diagnosis and Design for School Improvement* (with Coldren, Teachers College Press, 2011), *Distributed Leadership in Practice* (with Diamond, Teachers College Press, 2007), and *Distributed Leadership* (Jossey-Bass, 2006).

Louise Stoll is professor of education at the London Centre for Leadership in Learning, Institute of Education, University of London. Her research, R&D projects, and international consultancy focus on how schools, districts, and national systems create capacity for learning and improvement. Author of many publications translated into several languages, her recent titles include "Connecting Learning Communities" in the *Second International Handbook of Educational Change* (Springer, 2010) and *Professional Learning Communities: Divergence, Depth and Dilemmas* (with Louis, Open University Press, 2007).

Esteban Torre is advisor to the general executive director of Conectar Igualdad, Silvina Gvirtz, in Buenos Aires, Argentina. Prior to this position, he served as a political advisor to the Minister of Education of Buenos Aires. He holds a master's in Education from the Universidad de San Andres and a BA in Political Science from Universidad Torcuato di Tella.

Yong Zhao is the presidential chair and associate dean for Global Education, College of Education at the University of Oregon, and a fellow of the International Academy for Education. His most recent books include *World Class Learners: Educating Creative and Entrepreneurial Students* (Corwin, 2012), *Handbook of Asian Education: A Cultural Perspective* (Routledge, 2010), and *Catching Up or Leading the Way: American Education in the Age of Globalization* (ASCD, 2009).

Index